The Little Book
of Love Magic

Also by Sarah Bartlett

The Little Book *of* Love Magic

Sarah Bartlett

PIATKUS

PIATKUS

First published in Great Britain in 2023 by Piatkus

1 3 5 7 9 10 8 6 4 2

Copyright © 2023 Sarah Bartlett
Illustrations copyright © 2023 Sarah Bartlett

The moral right of the author has been asserted.

A CIP catalogue record for this book
is available from the British Library.

ISBN 978-0-3494-3327-1

Typeset in Perpetua by M Rules
Printed and bound in Great Britain by Clays Ltd, Elcograf S.p.A.

Papers used by Piatkus are from well-managed forests
and other responsible sources.

MIX
Paper from
responsible sources
FSC® C104740

Piatkus
An imprint of
Little, Brown Book Group
Carmelite House
50 Victoria Embankment
London EC4Y 0DZ

An Hachette UK Company
www.hachette.co.uk

www.littlebrown.co.uk

'To love is to burn, to be on fire.'

Sense and Sensibility, JANE AUSTEN

Contents

PART THREE
Universal and Mystical Love

Introduction

Poets, writers, artists, mystics and musicians throughout history have attempted to express, define, personify or depict the mysterious essence of love. One of the greatest writers among this number was English playwright William Shakespeare. The word 'love' appears over two thousand times in his plays and sonnets, and his works remain some of the most popular evocations of romantic feeling – quoted in everything from marriage speeches to Hollywood films. Romeo and Juliet's tragic love story looms large in our collective imagination while the romantic entanglements of *Twelfth Night* have been revisited time and time again on stage and screen, and Hamlet's proclamation of love for Ophelia passionately articulates true devotion: 'Doubt thou the stars are fire; Doubt that the sun doth move; Doubt truth to be a liar; But never doubt I love.' Whether we love with unconditional belief, experience the highs and lows of an intense relationship, or simply take the time to love our authentic self, we will all feel this magical energy touch us at some point in our lives.

If love really does make the world go round, then this book aims to align you with its essence so that you can glide through life, buoyed by its power. By encouraging self-confidence, summoning success, nourishing friendships, improving relationships and mastering self-love, you can deepen your connection to your sacred self and discover the integral role love plays in all of our lives.

What Is Love?

To codify love is an impossible feat. There isn't a neat, universal definition that can satisfy everyone, but to my mind the magic of love is an archetypal essence of the universe – a force that flows through all things and manifests in different ways depending on our unique experiences. In the traditional Western perception of the world, individualism is encouraged. We see ourselves as separate to the world rather than as part of it and we perceive love as an emotion that we feel acutely and personally, rather than as cosmic energy. However, when we fall in love we go from 'me' and 'you' to 'us', united by our love for one another. This bond allows us to see beyond ourselves and become one, as Cathy says of Heathcliff in Emily Bronte's *Wuthering Heights*: '[He is] more myself than I am. Whatever our souls are made of, his and mine are the same.'

Love comes to us in many forms, be it romantic, platonic, familial, gentle, passionate – and although not every relationship will stand the test of time, allowing love to blossom in our hearts enables our growth. If we want our life to be suffused with love's energy forever, we need to accept its nuances and understand how its different energies flow through us and how they can work beneficial magic for us.

We have individual needs, desires, ways of loving and being loved, but we are all touched by love's essence – and it is this very force that has promoted universal affinity throughout history.

Now let's take a brief look at some of the most evocative ways of perceiving love before you get to work with its magic and truly appreciate its power.

Love in the Ancient World

Ancient Greece was one of the most innovative civilisations of the ancient world, producing the finest philosophical thinkers and offering radical new approaches to subjects including art, science, politics and family. In fact, this vibrant culture lay the foundations for the way that life and love are still perceived in the Western world.

Love was such a complex and important part of ancient Greek civilisation that philosophers such as Plato and Aristotle developed their own ideas about it (see pages 6–7), while it was traditionally believed that 'love' could take six equal forms:

Philautia – love of the self
Eros – physical lust, desire, romance and passion
Philia – non-physical, kindred spirit, friendship
Pragma – longstanding love between partners
Agape – unconditional love for all
Storge – family love

Philautia – love of the self

We are all beginning to take the idea of self-care more seriously, realising that it isn't about being selfish, but a pathway towards self-understanding. In ancient Greece, healthy self-love or compassion for oneself was believed to be at the root of one's ability to truly love others. So before you can begin to be a truly loving friend, you need to be kind to yourself. You need to value who you are, respect your authentic self and lower your expectations of yourself and others.

Eros – passionate love and romance

This kind of love arouses sexual and romantic desire. It can be obsessive, but mostly it is passionate, binding you to another physically and emotionally. Our boundaries are broken down, we fall head over heels and we can't stop our feelings from running wild. We feel possessed, consumed by infatuation, addicted to love.

Eros was thought to be a dangerous type of love because, in excess, it could lead to the most obsessive love of all: 'mania'. Erotic love is thought to last from merely a few days to a few years, but it eventually burns out. This kind of intense relationship is difficult to maintain, and either the relationship will end, or it transforms into a deeper form of love, made up of Philia and Pragma.

Philia – friendship

To the ancient Greeks, love between friends was just as important as romantic love. This type of love later became known as platonic, after Plato wrote extensively about the bond between friends. Philia love is a connection between two minds, people who share similar experiences, beliefs or opinions, or who can accept each other's individual differences. There is no romantic or physical intention, but a sense of being with a kindred spirit, a friend who doesn't judge you, but loves you for who you are. Often, Philia develops in a long-term relationship but can precede a romantic relationship too.

Pragma – abiding love, acceptance

This is the love that has usually grown between two people in a long-term relationship. It is about tolerance, acceptance of the other's faults (although sometimes the couple are no longer aware of each other's weaknesses or strengths). This love is both affectionate, but also support-ive and forgiving. The longer a couple have been together, the better equipped they are to accept, understand and compromise to maintain a healthy relationship.

Agape – spiritual, unconditional love

A selfless, spiritual, unconditional love for others, often experienced as an all-embracing universal love flowing within oneself. In Christian belief, agape became associ-ated with the highest form of the love of God. Agape is a love that doesn't judge, doesn't set boundaries, conditions or expectations, and is empathetic, kind, compassionate, giving and forgiving.

Storge – family love

An affectionate love between family members, it is mostly experienced as the love between parents and their children, siblings, or family friends and relations. This love builds a sense of shared security and support. Storge is also the sense of belonging we feel when we find a group of like-minded people, or the shared pride in a belief system, a country, a clan.

The Philosophy of Love

At the heart of the expanding Greek civilisation was Athens, which became an intellectual hub for philosophers who wanted to exchange ideas and further their understanding of humanity. In the fourth century BC, Plato founded a school known as 'the Academy' to teach logic and reason and encourage radical new ways of thinking. Plato had been influenced by his own teacher, the great thinker Socrates, and in his new role at the Academy, he would go on to teach Aristotle, another philosopher who shaped the way we look at the world.

Plato's philosophy of love

Plato's work *The Symposium* is a philosophical dialogue set at a banquet, involving impromptu speeches from well-known historical figures, led by Socrates. These dialogues are mostly in praise of Eros, the Greek god of love and sexual desire. Both Eros and Plato's approaches to love are discussed at length and from numerous perspectives. Each invitee recounts a love story intended to convey to the others their particular argument for the philosophical stance.

Through the contesting participants, Plato presents the love of beauty and wisdom as the highest form of love. The only female invitee, the priestess Diotima, invokes the concept of the 'Ladder of Love'. This metaphor describes the steps of love that are taken to reach spiritual love and divine wisdom. The first rung of the ladder refers to initial attraction to physical beauty and sexual urges, which once transcended leads to love that encompasses an appreciation of the beauty of the mind, and finally to the love of beauty and divine wisdom.

Aristotle's philosophy of love

Aristotle believed that self-love is essential if you want to love others. He said:

> a man's best friend is the one who not only wishes him well but wishes it for his own sake (even though nobody will ever know it): and this condition is best fulfilled by his attitude towards himself – and similarly with all the other attributes that go to define a friend. For we have said before that all friendly feelings for others are extensions of a man's feelings for himself.

But ancient wisdom aside, there is another dance that love has led us through the centuries and this is best seen through the lens of mythology, where love was personified as a deity and whose archetypal myths and stories are as valid today as they were thousands of years ago.

Running alongside this has always been the use of the ubiquitous magic spell, the mainstay of any sorcerer or witch's grimoire when conjuring lust and love in an individual's heart.

Myth and Magic

There are numerous legends and myths throughout the world concerning love, simply because love is an enduring, persistent, motivating force in human life. Myth is the carrier of our collective need to know who we are; the psychologist Carl Jung called mythical archetypes 'great dreams of humanity', and that 'we have recollected ourselves from the Universe'. In fact, myths shape the way we view the world, and inform us of stories that are common to us all. Each of us is living our own myth, and love in its many forms is central to the story we tell ourselves and share with the world.

Here's a brief look at three ancient Greek and Roman mythological deities who have become iconic personifications of the Western concept of romantic love:

EROS (GREEK) / CUPID (ROMAN)
Originally a primordial god in the earliest creation myths according to Hesiod, Eros appeared with Tartarus and Earth and was born out of Chaos. Not only was he a force of nature, he was also an ancient and powerful phallic deity. He later appeared as the offspring of Aphrodite and Ares in the Olympic pantheon and was identified as the personification

of sexual desire. The ancient Greeks believed that if you were struck by one of Eros' arrows, you would be destined to fall in love. The symbolic association of love with arrows remains prevalent today, with Eros' Roman counterpart, Cupid, becoming synonymous with romance.

APHRODITE (GREEK) / VENUS (ROMAN)

When we think of love in the ancient world, perhaps the first person to come to mind is Aphrodite, the best-known love goddess of all. Love was personified in the beauty, vanity, sensuality and grace of the goddess, who was worshipped as Venus in the Roman tradition.

Aphrodite's lovers were numerous – from the gods of Olympus to sailors, soldiers and beautiful young men. Although married to Hephaestus, the dull and ugly god of fire and the forge, Aphrodite was besotted with Ares, the god of war. When Ares discovered she was having an affair with the beautiful youth Adonis, some claimed Ares disguised himself as a boar and killed his rival. Despite being a passionate lover, Aphrodite was also quick to bring misfortune on those who neglected her, cursing them with insatiable sexual desire – such as Phaedra, who was stricken with uncontrollable passion for her stepson Hippolytus, and Pasiphae, Queen of Crete, who lusted after the Cretan bull.

ZEUS (GREEK) / JUPITER (ROMAN)

The highly promiscuous god of the heavens, Zeus (later known as Jupiter in Roman mythology) was known to have chased after mortals, nymphs and goddesses alike.

Zeus was perhaps a mere instrument of 'physical love', who fathered a whole pantheon of deities, heroes and children, many of whom, such as Apollo, Artemis, the Muses, Persephone and Athena, were conceived through his love affairs with mortals such as Semele, Europa, Io and Leda. In his insatiable appetite, he was magical indeed! As a shapeshifter, he transformed into a shower of gold, a lightning rod, a swan, a flame and even a serpent to trick and seduce his intended love victim.

Love Magic

Love has also been the major influence in the grimoires of magi, sorcerers and witches, or those who were called upon to curse, bless, attract or lure love into our hearts. From ancient Egypt where the goddess of magic, Isis, restored Osiris to life by making love to him, to the medieval courtly love poems sang by troubadours, and the poetry, art and literature of nineteenth-century romantics, love as a source of inspiration is undeniable – and our enduring fascination with it shows the mysterious bewitching effect it has on us all.

A long time ago, as far back as the Palaeolithic period, the natural world was respected and plants, animals, rocks and stones were used to heal, cure or protect. The world and its natural phenomena were honoured, and this began a long tradition, in most cultures, of correspondences between the sky, weather, herbs, plants, animals, the planets, nature spirits and pantheons of gods.

Over the centuries, magic spells and incantations were used to stir passion or lust and to attract a lover; herbs and botanicals became tried and tested cures for love-sickness, or to bind a lover to you; crystals were worn or carried to promote goodness, to enhance all forms of spiritual love, protect and nurture the self; the planets, gods and goddesses were propitiated, and called on as oracles, revealing the outcomes of one's love choices, or divining future lovers and marriages.

The Greek Magic Papyri

A collection of ancient magic spells, rituals and charms for love can be found in the body of texts known as the Greek Magical Papyri, mostly written between 100 BCE and 400 CE in Graeco-Roman Egypt. The papers contain recipes, folk remedies, curse tablets, love charms and talismans, and a large number of cures for impotence. Most of this erotic magic literature was made up of binding, attraction and cursing spells. Here are some examples:

One spell recounts how to seduce a woman with a mussel by painting the figure of Typhon (a monster cast into the underworld by Zeus) onto the shell. Then, with myrrh ink, you wrote Typhon's name around the image and dropped the mussel into a bathhouse furnace. As you did so, you repeated Typhon's name, along with the name of the woman you wished to enflame with desire, and it was believed that she would then very soon appear in your life (although hopefully not in the bathhouse fire!)

In one text, ascribed to Hermes, apples were suggested as a method to attract a lover. They were believed to be powerful tools to promote love as they were sacred to Aphrodite, and as such you would be drawing on the power of the goddess of love herself.

Many of the erotic attraction spells include the practice of 'drawing down the moon', along with the clashing of cymbals (the sound was thought to resonate to the moon's energy and thereby bring it to you directly). Drawing down the moon in a less literal way is still a common feature of modern-day Wiccan and other pagan magical spells. Carrying an amulet was also a popular way to attract a lover, and these were often carved with empowering symbols, such as intaglios of the lovers Eros and Psyche.

Medieval Love Recipes

By the medieval period, magic was predominantly used to seduce, improve or facilitate better sex between a couple, to keep a lover from straying, or to disrupt or break up a love affair. Carved amulets and charms were the most common exchanges between lovers, such as the many talismans featuring Harpocrates, the Greek god of silence and secrets, who remained a powerful influence in the folklore of the medieval period. Carved on green jasper, the god was usually depicted sitting on a lotus flower, and the charm was worn or carried to ensure a love tryst was kept secret.

Obscure magical recipes and ingredients have been found in many medieval pharmaceutical texts, such as the work of Marcellus of Bordeaux, a fifth-century CE physician. His extensive text was filled with remedies, herbal cures and aphrodisiacs, using anything from cloves and cinnamon to land snails and worms. His compendium of pharmacological preparations, *De medicamentis*, included a cure for boosting a man's sex drive by wearing the testicle of a rooster in a pouch around his neck! Many of these love charms were engraved with magical sigils (signs and symbols), or incantations known as *voces magicae*, as well as palindromes, images or names of gods, demons and other supernatural beings.

By the time of the first witch hunts, folk remedies, magical cures and midwives were deemed heretical, and the Christian Church presided over Europe. Yet folk love magic was undeterred, and the most macabre recipes for curing, hindering or inducing love went underground. Magical spells continued to be in demand for inciting love in others and were usually made up of a mix of botanicals, bones and animal entrails. For example, in grimoires such as the eighteenth-century *The Petit Albert*, readers were encouraged to mix vervain, known as the herb of enchantment, with beetle wings and honey, while worms were peppered with powdered periwinkle, and gruesome animal remains were blended with rose water. In love spells, the two most important ingredients were menstrual blood and pubic hair, which were incorporated into potions, talismans and powders to induce, seduce and invoke erotic love.

This kind of magic started as a way to elicit guidance and encouragement from a higher power, but evolved into a way of manipulating the cosmos so a person could take control of their own destiny. Magi, sorcerers, witches and seers all worked with these symbols and correspondences to invoke the powers of nature and the divine to ensure the favour of the gods and the planets (and of course, to make a profitable business out of one's dilemma!).

Nowadays, magic is about making the things you want to happen a reality, not only for the good of yourself, but also for the universe. However, you truly have to believe in magic for it to work.

Love is a mystery to be lived, and it is through this magic that we can bestow love's gift to all.

Using This Book

Before you begin, reflect on two things:

First, that what you are doing is for the good of the universe, and that you truly *believe* in magic. If you don't believe in magic it won't work because intention and belief are the keys to connecting to universal energy.

Second, according to the law of magic, what goes around comes around, and usually threefold. In other words, when you send out your intentions with true belief, they must also be sent with goodness for all. So never perform rituals in a moment of impulse, or in anger or to hurt or upset others. Every time you perform a ritual, think about your motives: are they prompted by goodwill and true loving kindness for everyone and everything in the universe?

All the rituals, spells and enchantments included in this book are aimed at deepening your connection to your sacred self and improving all forms of love relationships. By using magic, you can welcome the mysterious quality of love into your life to not only benefit from its care, but radiate love out to the planet, to make it a loving, pro-tected place too.

In the first part of this book, you will discover rituals and practices to honour and inspirit self-love and care for who you are, ways to enhance the sensual you, and how to be true to who you really are and manifest your authentic self. The second part is filled with rituals for attracting romance, healing love's illusions, improving or encouraging long-term relationships, and caring for platonic and familial bonds. Finally, the last part will offer ways to connect with and love the universe and all that's in it. This kind of divine love will nurture your soul and allow you to feel at one with nature.

You can use this book in any way you like, be it dipping in and out or working through section by section. But I would suggest beginning your magical journey with one of the first two rituals in the next chapter for invoking 'self-belief' and for 'feeling the warmth of love', so you really get to know what love is all about – within you, and all around you.

Please note: I have used a variety of specific botanicals, stones, crystals, candles and other ingredients, but if you can't get hold of any of these, substitute with any of the corresponding ingredients listed in the glossary at the end of this book.

Using candles: using lit candles can cause fires, so please take great care to keep them away from any flammable materials, and always blow them out safely at the end of any ritual.

If you prefer NOT to light candles for safety reasons, then use a simple visualisation technique instead. All you need to do is imagine yourself lighting the candle, then watching the candle flame burning before you, and remember to visualise blowing the flame out at the end of the ritual too! Lighting and extinguishing candles is a powerful ritualistic gesture for sealing intentions in many love spells.

PART ONE

Love of Self

'Self-love, my liege, is not so vile a
sin as self-neglecting.'

Henry V, William Shakespeare

What Is Self-Love?

We are all becoming more aware about how important it is to look after our physical and mental wellbeing. But in the world of magic, self-love goes a little further than self-care. In fact, loving oneself is not only taking responsibility for who we are as individuals and caring about that self, but actually creating positive and magical energy around us to improve, enhance or maximise our unique potential, and to project this out to the world. In order to love ourselves fully and deeply, we need to embrace the parts of us that we keep hidden or neglect. We need to be radically honest and true to who we are at our core.

In the following section you will find rituals, spells and other magic that will help you to master self-love. It's not just about waving a magic wand and hey presto, you suddenly become a self-loving, good person, who says, 'I love myself so it's OK to be me.' Yes, you need to make that affirmation, but it's meaningless unless you truly feel the love within you.

Increasingly we're recognising the importance and power of self-love as a concept, but it wasn't always this way. In the seventeenth century, a number of 'enlightened' French philosophers, namely Pascal and La Rochefoucauld, decided that self-love was vanity, and involved favouring oneself at the expense of others. They believed it was based on the individual need to feed off society's approval to give one a sense of self-esteem – this they referred to as '*l'amour propre*'. This aggrandised sense of self is similar to that of arrogance and conceit.

In the eighteenth century, Rousseau – a slightly more forgiving French philosopher – proposed the idea of *amour de soi*. He aligned this to a more primitive sense of self-love that didn't arise from our relationship with others, but from an animal survival instinct. If we look at his idea through esoteric eyes, then this is the kind of love that might be closer to loving one's magical 'self' and its connection to the universe.

So for our purposes, love of self encompasses:

- Loving who you are
- Engaging in and expressing the potentials within yourself
- Honouring your sacred self
- Living a life where you can be authentic
- Being true to your individuality
- Self-acceptance and self-understanding
- Feeling a sense of your connection with nature

The rituals and practices in this section will help you to nurture and nourish your authentic self, celebrate your strengths, encourage acceptance, invoke self-understanding and cultivate kindness.

There are also chapters of spells and rituals for understanding your feelings and emotions; about embracing the sensual witch inside you, and how it's all right to have desires; how it's also all right not to have to achieve or prove anything. There are also rituals for self-protection from geopathic (negative environmental energy) and psychic stress, and how to nurture self-empowerment for success, motivation and manifestation.

So rather than beat yourself up, love yourself up.

Chapter One

Nurturing Who You Are

'It is better to be hated for what
you are than to be loved for what
you are not.'

André Gide

The following practices, rituals and spells are designed to
help you nurture, love, restore and inspirit 'you', because
you deserve everything that the world has to offer. In
order to show up for, and take care of, the people around
you, it's important that you also take time to focus on your

own wellbeing and appreciate the wonderful person that you are. Even if there are moments where you might doubt yourself or feel that you're lacking, you can overcome them by developing a deep appreciation for who you are.

Before you work your way through the rituals in this chapter, I would encourage you to try the next two exercises to help boost your self-belief and connect you to love's magical energy. These exercises can be repeated daily to keep the positive energy flowing.

RITUAL TO AWAKEN SELF-BELIEF

Affirming to yourself that you are confident, positive and sure of your motives on a daily basis is a great way to gradually build up belief in who you are and your unique purpose. This magic ritual will bring clarity and instil confidence. Belief is everything – it shapes our lives, dreams and desires. Believing in magic is one thing, but believing in the magic of yourself is also the key to loving yourself – flaws and all.

You will need:
3 x 2ft lengths of gold ribbon or twine
3 keys
3 pieces of citrine
a white tea-light candle

1. Light the candle and place the three keys in a triangular formation. Then place each of the citrine crystals next to a key.

2. Knot the three ribbons together at one end, then make a knot in the middle and one more at the opposite end, repeating the following as each knot is made: 'I knot into my life the three keys of trust, confidence and acceptance of who I am.'

3. Form a circle around your triangle with the knotted ribbons, repeating as you do: 'These three keys will bring me self-belief so I can flourish and become true to myself.'

4. Blow out the candle and place the three keys and the citrine in a safe place. Resolve to start each day by holding a piece of citrine for a few minutes to reinforce personal integrity.

FEELING THE WARMTH OF LOVE

To connect to the warmth of love and to nurture and let it come to you, perform this ritual every day if possible. See this as a little 'treat', a mindful moment of gratitude for being who you are.

You will need:
a piece of rose quartz or rhodochrosite

1. Settle down somewhere calm where you can be alone. Hold the crystal in your hands to your navel,

close your eyes and clear your mind. Visualise the energy of love and acceptance flowing through you to the deepest part of yourself. (Maybe imagine 'love' as the pink crystal itself, to give it some tangible form if you find it hard to visualise an abstract concept).

2. The love is flowing through you, warming and energising every inch of your body, perhaps moving around your chakras (see page 117 and 243), until it comes to rest in your soul. This is the soul that forgives and forgets, the soul that profoundly accepts the love that is given, and the love you have to give. Hold the stone for a few more minutes until you experience a sense that you are radiating love and yet drawing it to you, as if you are a conduit for love as it flows through you, permeating all of your being.

3. Come out of your visualisation and place the crystal on a flat surface and affirm your love of the crystal, because it is now empowered not only with universal love, but with your love too.

4. Keep the crystal with you, and whenever you need to feel love for yourself, hold it tightly in your hand or place it close to your chest.

5. Getting in touch with this soulful loving place means you will begin to experience a deeper sense of loving who you are too.

SHINE LIKE THE SUN RITUAL

One of the things that affects many of us is a lack of confidence in our own ability. We might tell ourselves that we're not deserving or that we're simply not good enough, but if we repeat the same old negative self-talk, we'll never be able to flourish. Gently opening the door to a world of possibility and belief will allow your self-confidence to gradually develop. So if something goes wrong today, don't beat yourself up about it – instead be kind. As I keep repeating, unless you start to love yourself (faults, insecurities and all), you won't be very good at appreciating or caring about what other people might need.

Perform this ritual whenever you feel you lack confidence, or feel a twinge of guilt for putting yourself first. Becoming self-aware and honest with yourself is the key to shining like the sun.

You will need:
a mirror (propped up)
5 pink candles
5 sunflower seeds
A clear quartz crystal

1. To begin, find a flat surface that you can use to carry out this ritual. Place the mirror in the centre of the surface and then position your quartz in front of it. Form a circle around the quartz with the five candles and then light each candle. Put the five seeds in a line in front of the candles. Gaze at

the candle flames in the mirror for a minute or so, to find stillness.

2.   Then pick up each seed in turn and hold in your hand as you say:

'Like the sun I shine my best,
When cloudless skies reveal my quest,
These seeds will sow awareness true
And bring me faith in all I do.'

3.   Focus on yourself for a minute, and see yourself as radiant as the sun, ready to spring into life like sunflower seeds. Then blow out the candles, and sprinkle the seeds over the crystal to seal your intention to put yourself first.

4.   Leave your petition in place over night, and then keep the crystal in a safe place until you need to repeat the ritual to restore self-awareness.

A RITUAL FOR AUTHENTIC SELF-ENCHANTMENT

Gaining objective insight into the bits of you that make up the whole means you can begin to be kind to yourself. OK, you have faults, everyone does, but you don't need to beat yourself up about them, or try to change anything, unless of course you're intending to improve or turn negativity into positive qualities. This little ritual is about being honest with yourself to discover the authentic you, so you can work with all your qualities to make your life more fulfilling.

You will need:
a piece of paper and a pen
a box with a lid
a handful of lavender flowers
a piece of black obsidian (for clarity and removing negativity)
a piece of rutilated quartz (for truth and self-realisation)

1. Hold the two crystals, one in each hand, and focus for a while on your quest for discovering your authentic self. Then place them on the table, and sprinkle the lavender flowers over them.

2. Ask yourself the following questions one by one, and write down your answers to each one on your piece of paper.

   • What makes me feel fulfilled?
   • What do I feel I lack?
   • What motivates me?
   • What impact do I want to make on the world?
   • What is my biggest fault?
   • What is my greatest gift?
   • Who am I?

3. Don't worry if you don't have an answer for every question, because we don't always have all the answers. It's more important to be truthful and

sometimes that means admitting, 'Hey, I don't know the answer to that.' Finally, note down the following affirmation: 'I am being true to my authentic self, and will discover and honour the truth of who I am. I am worthy of self-love and the love of others.'

4. Fold up the paper afterwards, place it in your box with the crystals and flowers, and whenever you need to reconnect again with your authentic self, you can review your statements and make note of anything that's changed.

A Ritual for Conjuring Confidence

Confidence allows us to feel comfortable in our own skin and appreciate our unique magic, so that we can move through the world with ease. This simple ritual will instil a sense of heartfelt confidence in yourself. The more confident you are, the more you can start to trust and love yourself, without relying on external praise or approval to feel worthy.

You will need:
2 red tea-light candles
a piece of red carnelian
a piece of citrine
a sunstone
cedarwood essential oil
an image of a sunrise

This ritual is preferably carried out on the evening of a waxing moon.

1. Place the image of your sunrise on a flat surface, then place the two red candles on either side of the image. Light the candles, making sure to be careful as you do so.
2. Hold the red carnelian in your hands and gaze into the candle flames as you say: 'With red my courage lights the sun, to bring me spirit, now it's done.'
3. Next pick up the citrine and say: 'With yellow gold my poise is set, just like this sun my soul is blessed.'
4. Finally, hold up the sunstone and say: 'The sun and moon by love's own sake, have filled me now with utter faith.'
5. To seal your intention to gain more confidence, drip a drop of the cedarwood oil onto each of your crystals, then place them in a triangle shape around the sunrise image. Be mindful for a few minutes of your intention, and how the sunrise shines between the flames, reminding you of your own inner light awakened, confident, and filling you with self-esteem. Don't forget to blow out the candles.

A Ritual to Embrace Your Flaws

Sometimes it can be difficult to fully embrace the parts of ourselves that we label as flawed or unattractive. When we talk about ourselves, it's often easy to focus on the things we like, for example we might say 'Yes, I'm a great communicator', but we're less likely to admit, 'I'm quick to anger', or 'I feel so mediocre'. Whatever concerns or 'flaws' you believe you have, this little ritual will help you to see them in a positive light by giving them a little love and attention.

You will need:
a jar with a lid
5 small pieces of paper and a pen
5 gold star stickers
a piece of lapis lazuli
ylang ylang essential oil

1. On each piece of paper, write a word for each inadequacy or flaw you think you have – you might not need or want to use all five pieces, just think of traits that you can cultivate into positives. For example, 'wasteful' can become 'economical'; 'irresponsible', 'responsible'; 'impatient', 'patient', and so on.
2. When you have finished, stick a star on each piece of paper – these are now your gold star faults.
3. Scatter them into your jar, drop in the five drops of ylang ylang essential oil and the piece of lapis lazuli. Stir with one finger for ten seconds to let

the magic work, then without looking, pull out one piece of paper.

4. Read your flaw, and say: 'I embrace this flaw, and accept it is part of my persona, but from now on will be mindful of it, either by transforming it from a vice to a virtue or accepting my gold star will one day be a truly loved star in the sky.'

5. Then for the next few days keep reviewing this particular trait. When you find that your attitude is slowly changing, or that you've started taking accountability for why you act this way, throw away the paper and move onto the next, until your jar is empty.

6. By accepting these flaws, or attempting to flip them into positive qualities, you are truly giving them some loving attention.

Wants and Needs

There are two more questions you have to ask yourself before you can really start to care deeply for all of you. What do I *want* to learn to love about myself? What do I *need* to learn to love about myself?

Want implies 'lack'. When we are 'wanting' it is because we don't have whatever it is we believe we lack. Often, we perceive ourselves to be lacking, if we look around and compare our own experience to that of a friend or family member. It can be simply, 'I want to be married', or 'I want a new car'.

Need can also imply a sense of lack, but it's also more visceral. A need is something that feels absolutely essential to our wellbeing.

Both want and need are things we 'attach' ourselves to throughout life, and are part of being human – but do you ever stop to consider what you need to learn to love about yourself and what you want to learn to love about yourself?

A Ritual to Nurture Self-Worth

Perform this ritual preferably on the evening of a waxing moon.

You will need:
a piece of paper
a pen
5 pieces of malachite
bergamot essential oil
5 bay leaves
2 white tea-light candles

1. On your piece of paper, write down one thing you want to learn to love about yourself – perhaps it's a trait that you admire in a friend that you'd like to nurture in yourself.
2. Now write down what you need to learn to love about yourself. Remember this should be based on necessity rather than desire – perhaps it's something you've felt self-conscious about in the

past, but that you now feel ready to embrace as a strength.

3. Place the candles either side of the paper statement, but don't light them.

4. Make a circle around the paper and candles by alternating five bay leaves with the five malachite crystals, all evenly spaced.

5. Anoint your paper with the bergamot oil, and as you drip a drop onto each crystal and leaf, repeat:

'Of want and need I take my share,
This love I give myself is fair,
In malachite I find my worth,
Of bay leaves wise I find my truth,
Take bergamot and drip desire
To bring me love and stoke my fire.'

6. Focus for a few minutes on what you want to love about yourself and what you need to love about yourself. Then remove the malachite and keep the piece of paper in a safe place until the full moon.

7. On the evening of the full moon light the two tea-light candles and repeat your 'want' and 'need' aloud, then blow out the candles to seal your intention to the universe. Within one lunar cycle you will begin to place more value on what you need to love about yourself and what you want to learn to love about yourself and promote a better sense of self-love.

A PASSION-SEEKING CHARM

Having a passion in life is uplifting, as it provides us with a sense of connection to our sacred self. This can be anything from a vocation to a hobby, or even a spiritual pursuit. But what makes this 'passion' special is that it's completely absorbing and offers a sanctuary from the endless demands of modern life. While you're engaged in this activity, you have no cares, no worries, there is no sense of time and you are at one with the moment. This pathway to 'passion' will enable you to feel love from within as well as from without.

The enchantment draws on the energy of the Greek god of light, Apollo, who travelled across the sky by day in a golden chariot bringing passion, light and inspiration to the world.

Perform this ritual in the morning on a sunny day.

You will need:
5 gold rings
5 x 2ft lengths of gold ribbon or cord
5 sunstones or goldstones

1. Place the five crystals in a circle. Take each length of material and make five equidistant knots along each, and then thread each ribbon through a gold ring, tying the ends together to seal your intention to discover passion.
2. Surround each crystal with a ribboned ring, and as you do say:

*'With five gold rings and ribbons gold
I thread my way to passion's soul,
These crystals call Apollo's sight
To see my way and find true light.'*

3. Leave everything in place over the course of the day, before removing at sunset and storing in a safe, secret place. Within one lunar cycle, you will have taken steps towards discovering your true passion.

OPENING YOURSELF UP TO LOVE

Before you go deeper into your feelings, banishing negativity and embracing change, you need to open yourself up to love's magical force with the symbolic and empowering energy of Venus.

This is the first of two rituals involving renaissance painter Botticelli's mythological allegories, which are both embedded with enchantment in their symbols and magical allusions. (The second is on page 46.)

Botticelli's *The Birth of Venus* is an iconic depiction of a newly born Aphrodite/Venus. When the severed genitals of Ouranos fell to the sea following an attack on the primordial god at the hand of his son Cronus, Aphrodite sprang fully formed from the sea foam. Blown across the ocean by the west wind, Zephyros, Aphrodite came to rest on dry land. Here's how to invite a little of her loving essence into your own world.

You will need:
an image of a dove
a conch shell (or image of one)
a mirror
a pink candle
a single terminator quartz crystal
2 pieces of rose quartz

1. Sit in a comfortable position in front of the mirror. Place the candle in front of you and carefully light it. Find stillness as you gaze into the flame or the reflection of the flame in the mirror.
2. Take the conch shell and place it in front of the candle, with a piece of rose quartz on either side of the shell. Then repeat: 'With Venus' power I welcome love from ocean's shells and wings of dove.'
3. Now place the image of the dove before you and the clear quartz terminator on top of it, with the point facing towards you, directing the essence of love your way.
4. Turn your attention to the image of the shell and, holding a piece of rose quartz in each hand, repeat:

'With rose quartz now this love is found,
She's welcome here, her wings unbound
When now this candle blown will be,
And goddess love bestowed on me.'

5. As you blow out your candle, imagine you are the west wind, blowing Venus gently on to dry land and to safety. Visualise this energy radiating all around you, as it passes through the crystals, they are touched by this power.

Welcoming love in this way means that it will always find its way to flow to you, whenever you need to call on its magic.

LETTING LOVE SETTLE IN

Now that you have welcomed love and can let it come to you freely, when you need to summon a little self-care energy, here's how to let it settle in and stay a while, as if it were moving into a warm, cosy home, where all is safe and welcoming. Love stays where the fires are stoked, where the home is protected, and where there's no tension or anger. It is the energies of negativity, fear and manipulation that send love scuttling out the door.

Here's how to ensure love stays for as long as you want it to.

The virgin goddess of the hearth and home, Hestia, was also goddess of the sacrificial flame of the gods. In her role as protector and guardian of the fire, she was called upon to bring comfort, wellbeing and protection to the household, similarly you can help love settle into your own home by recreating Hestia's hearth.

You will need:

a tall red candle
10 red tea-light candles
4 roses (or images of roses)
3 rough rubies or garnets
a drink of your choice

1. Find a special place in your home where you can set up your love hearth (when choosing a spot, bear in mind that the hearth will need to stay in place for one lunar cycle). Your taller candle will form the centrepiece of the hearth, so place the ten tea-lights around it to form a circle.
2. To the north, south, east and west of the circle, place the four roses.
3. Take two of your rough stones and gently position them on either side of your north rose. Then place your final stone beneath your south rose.
4. Now go back and light all of the candles. For the next few minutes, observe the flickering flames and try to find stillness.
5. Then repeat:

   'With Hestia, my home is set
   For joyful love and no regrets,
   Where heart and hearth are filled with warmth
   And love can find a place unworn;
   Then love can come and settle here,
   To nestle in my hearth so dear.
   Now oils and roses bring me light,

To sanction love and give her life,
Within these walls where rubies dance
To stoke the fire, and love enchant.'

6. When you feel ready, blow out the candles. Then take up one of your stones, whichever calls to you, and hold it close to your heart. Close your eyes and sense love settling in.

7. Keep this sacred stone by your bed. Leave the love hearth in its place for at least one lunar cycle to activate the energy for love to stay in your home and heart.

8. Now that you've discovered how to let love permeate your world, the next chapter shows you some special ways to care for your feelings, desires and to promote self-understanding and awareness.

Chapter Two

Cultivating Self-Awareness and Encouraging Self-Esteem

'To love oneself is the beginning of a lifelong romance.'

Oscar Wilde

We all share similar traits, feelings and qualities, but we all express, experience or characterise these in different ways, depending on our unique individuality. In astrological circles, the moment in time we are born is reflected by the planets in the sky, and this unique blueprint, known as the horoscope, indicates how we are most likely to express ourselves throughout our life journey. We will be looking at how to utilise this knowledge in the section on vocation (see page 74). By understanding which qualities we express more or less, we can also begin to understand the people around us as individuals, learn to accept others and be more loving and understanding of differences too.

This chapter uses rituals and practices to enhance your sense of being 'centred' – in other words finding a balance between 'self-centredness' (too much ego) and 'self-consciousness' (too little ego) by offering ways to establish and promote self-awareness and self-esteem. It also looks at ways to protect and nurture you against outer negativity and inner stresses, not forgetting embracing your creativity, imagination, desires and more.

BEING CENTRED, WITHOUT BEING SELF-CENTRED

When we say someone is self-centred, we imply they care more about themselves than others, but that doesn't have to be the case. Here's how to find balance and awareness by engaging with the second of Botticelli's paintings used in this book, *Primavera,* so that you can feel centred within yourself. This ritual will ensure that you are the focus of your greatest work of art: you.

Primavera is believed to be constructed in such a way that there is a symbolic balance of the main elements of human nature. The general interpretation of this iconic painting is that the figure to the right is the wind, Zephyros, who lusts after the nymph Chloris. Once the nymph is possessed by the wind god, she is transformed into the goddess of spring, Flora. The female figure in the middle of the painting is usually identified as Venus, accompanied by the three Graces, while to the left Mercury raises his caduceus (a magic wand) to clear the clouds from the sky. All is set in an allegorical orange grove, a motif of the powerful Medici family, who likely commissioned this painting for a forthcoming marriage.

You will need:
an image of *Primavera*
a piece of paper and a pen
a piece of rose quartz
a pink tea-light candle

1. Study the painting for a few minutes, note the way Chloris's lips 'breathe spring roses' according to Ovid, and while doing so she is literally being transformed into the gentle, smiling goddess Flora. Imagine yourself as a nymph who attempts to flee from the lusting wind and then, once his lover, as the goddess of spring.

2. Next, visualise yourself as Venus, who, in Roman myth, had become a kinder, pleasure-loving, gentle and beneficial goddess. Then imagine yourself as Mercury, the three Graces and Cupid hovering above.

3. On your piece of paper, write the following affirmations:

- I am like Zephyrus, desiring of others, but willing to breathe love into them
- I am like Chloris, desired and transformed by desire into the goddess of spring Flora
- I am like the three Graces, delighting in the world of nature
- I am like Mercury, able to see through the cloud's illusions
- I am like Cupid, giving my love to others
- I am centred not self-centred. I am like Venus herself, at the centre of this work of art.

4. Hold the rose quartz in your hands as you say aloud your affirmations.
5. Blow out the candle, fold your piece of paper with your affirmations around the image of the painting and then roll everything up into a scroll, securing it with a pink ribbon. Keep your scroll in a safe place, and this enchantment will bestow you with a beautifully centred self. Open it every full moon to remind you that you are at the centre of your own work of art.

Embracing Creativity

Creativity seems to arise from a place deep within us, perhaps indeed our soul. Whether we feel that creative urge to pick up a paintbrush, write a novel or simply work in the garden, whatever we produce is our personal 'work of art' (in all its forms). We feel good about our self, sometimes lose touch with 'reality' and enter another realm, timeless and carefree. However, there are moments when a niggling fear of failure or negative outcomes such as, 'I'm not good enough', or 'I'm too busy', create blockages rather than encouraging the fabulous blossoms of creative growth. Here's how to overcome that kind of barrier and also summon more creativity in your life. It shows you love and care for this hidden yet beautiful part of you.

You will need:
a red candle
a black candle
the Empress tarot card (represents creativity)
the Devil tarot card (represents blockage)
a piece of paper and a pen

1. Place the Devil card horizontally across the Empress card, with the red candle to the right and the black candle to the left.
2. Light the candles and write down your current creative intention – whether you feel capable of it or not.

3. Place the paper under the two tarot cards and rest your hand on the pile as you say:

    'The Devil may block me from making my way,
    But the Empress is there to show me the day.
    With this candle, intention is lit well and true,
    So snuff out the black one to bring me the new.'

4. Carefully blow out the black candle without blowing out the red, and then remove the Devil card and place it under the black candle. Now seal your intention to get creative by saying:

    'The Empress points the way to my goal, and I will now follow the creative joy I have expressed to the universe.'

5. Blow out the candle, leave in place overnight, and in the following days you will overcome any blockages and will be able to access the creative spirit within you.

Rejoicing in Inspiration with Herbs and Stones

Inspiration derives from the Latin *inspirare*, meaning to breathe into, and was believed to be the divine or mystical breath of the god of light, Apollo, who inspired nature and brought it to life. The landscape is filled with divine energy, and nature often acts as a source of inspiration and delight. It is this divine magic that will connect you to the very essence of Apollo's breath, so you can feel inspired and rejoice in yourself.

This ritual is best suited to sunny days.

You will need:
a walk in the countryside
a handful of small stones
a pouch of fresh mixed herbs (rosemary, thyme and sage)

1. Walk to a favourite scenic spot where you can be alone and can find stillness. When you get there, sit or stand for a few moments, as you reflect on and open your mind to the view before you. Then say:

   'With nature's gifts and Apollo's designs,
   I'm stirred to fill and lift my mind
   To greater thoughts for future goals,
   And draw on inspiration's soul.'

2. To seal your intention to be inspired by nature and Apollo's light, scatter your pouch of herbs, followed by the stones, and then gently cover them with natural vegetation.

3. Carry on being mindful of the world around you for a few minutes and let your mind wander through the landscape as you connect to nature's energy.

Use this little ritual whenever you're looking for fresh inspiration.

Summoning Success with the Full Moon

Armed with inspiration and creativity, now you can summon success to manifest your goals. Loving your goals is about loving yourself, because, after all, they are a manifestation of your personal desires.

Call on the empowering energy of the full moon to bring you a sizzling future.

You will need:
3 white roses (or images)
3 white candles
3 silver rings
a silver-coloured or white pouch
a 1ft length of silver ribbon or cord
sandalwood oil

1. On the evening of the full moon, place your candles in a horizontal row on a flat surface. Then carefully light each of the candles.
2. Take up the ribbon and thread on the silver rings, then tie the ends of the ribbon together to bind the rings.
3. Place the ribbon and rings in the pouch. Lay the pouch in front of the candles, before placing a rose to the south, east, and west of the pouch.

4. Drop a little of the sandalwood oil onto each flower, taking care to avoid the candles, and say:

> *'The lunar orb is mine this night,*
> *To turn ideas to treasures bright,*
> *To show me where success will be,*
> *And all rewards are shared with me,*
> *These silver rings and ribbon seal*
> *My best intents to make goals real.'*

5. With your finger draw an imaginary circle around the pouch in an anti-clockwise direction to symbolise your intention for success in manifesting your goals. Leave this in place overnight, then dispose of the flowers with care.
6. Carry the pouch with you, until the success you are seeking comes your way.

LOVING YOUR ACCOMPLISHMENTS WITH PRECIOUS OUD

Oud, also known as 'agarwood', is a highly prized perfume sourced from a species of tree found mostly in South East Asia. It has a musky, woody, earthy fragrance and is sometimes referred to as the 'liquid gold' of perfume. The real thing is quite rare and can be expensive, but you can buy manufactured oud, which is more economical and will minimise the over-farming of the trees and will work just as well for this spell.

The scent is unforgettable, so that when you associate your accomplishments with its mesmerising fragrance, they will remain at the forefront of your mind. You will love yourself and your achievements every time you take a whiff of this magical scent. Use this simple enchantment to boost your sense of attainment in anything you do, from learning a new skill, to feeling you are being true to yourself.

This ritual is best performed on the day of a waxing moon.

You will need:
3 small rough rubies
oud perfume or essential oil
a tree
a pouch

Once you have chosen your tree, make a dedicated journey with your ingredients to perform this ritual.

1. Stand before the tree and say: 'Thank you, tree, for showing me strength and accomplishment.'
2. Raise your palms and touch the bark for a minute or so, or just give the whole trunk a big hug. As you do so, imagine the strength and majesty of this tree giving you a big hug back.
3. Place the rubies on the ground in a horizontal line, and drizzle a little of the oud onto each crystal. Say:

   'Take precious oud and rubies raw,
   To make my life accomplished joy,

This tree will store intentions true,
And give me love for all I do.'

4. Now bury two of the rubies shallowly in the ground to show your love for planet Earth and to give root to your connection with the tree, keeping the final ruby for the pouch. Cover the sacred place with soil or weeds to consecrate your ritual.
5. Take the remaining ruby and hold it close to your nose to breathe in the musky fragrance of the oud to complete the ritual. Whenever you need to revive the joyful sense of accomplishment and reconnect to your precious oud experience, breathe in your ruby.

BANISHING INSECURITY

Many of us are self-conscious – in other words, we lack confidence in ourselves, our ego is a little tarnished, or we rely heavily on other people to feed our self-esteem. We are inhibited or unassertive, and may be nervous to stick up for our beliefs or desires. We may be people-pleasers by nature, drawing our sense of worth from pleasing everyone but ourselves. Or we may worry about what others may think of us: how do I look? Will anyone criticise me? If I do this, what will they say? And so on. If you fall into this category, or have any kind of inhibitions or insecurities, then here's a way to encourage balance and restore self-worth and esteem.

The four wind gods of Greek mythology – Zephyrus, Boreus, Notus and Eurus – will invite the right amount of confidence (Zephyrus, west wind and the spring), self-containment (Boreus, north wind and the winter), free-spiritedness (Notus, south wind and the summer), and self-assuredness (Eurus, the east and autumn) into your world, so you can begin to feel a more confident, self-reliant you.

You will need:
4 candles (one for each direction): red for south, blue for
    north, green for west and white for east
a clear quartz crystal

1. Place the four candles in their corresponding compass point positions around the crystal. Light them, and for a minute or so, focus on the quartz in the centre and say:

   'This self-made place is mine to be,
   Where winds blow strength and love is free.
   From north, south, west and the east too,
   Self-worth returns, no doubts or blues.
   I'm richer now with winds of change
   That show me how to sing again.'

2. Now blow out the candles one by one, as if directing the energy of each wind towards the quartz in the centre.

3. Now hold it close to your heart chakra (see page
   243) as you repeat the charm again.

You will feel uplifted and filled with a bold sense of
self-esteem. Repeat this ritual whenever you want to feel
a sense of security.

WISH ENCHANTMENT

In medieval Europe, nature spirits – whether water, tree
or earth nymphs, satyr or centaurs – were called upon
in the early summer to celebrate the waxing sun as it
made its way to the highest point in the sky. This natural
occurrence was seen as a symbol of growth and creativity and usually coincided with the Eve of Beltane on 30
April, when young maidens would make a wish to meet
their true love before the summer solstice that year. You
too can harness the power of this magical time and call
on the spirits of Fire, Earth, Water and Air (used in these
ancient rites of spring) to make a wish for a new project
or goal. You can perform this wish ritual any time of year
simply by creating a symbolic association with Beltane
and incorporating elemental energy through a pentagram
(a five-pointed star).

You will need:
a piece of paper and a pen
a red candle
5 pieces of citrine

5 pieces of rose quartz

1. Begin by drawing a large pentagram, while considering what it is that you want from the universe. Then draw a circle around your pentagram to seal your intention.
2. Place a piece of citrine in each of the pentagram's points, with a piece of the rose quartz between each point of the star.
3. In the middle place the unlit red candle to show your connection with the spirits of Fire.
4. To show your appreciation for Earth spirits, gently kiss each of your crystals in turn.
5. To connect to the spirits of Air, say:

   'Ten crystals give me love so dear,
   To manifest my thoughts so clear.'

6. Then, to call in the spirits of Water, say:

   'The rippling waters flowing down,
   Will bring my wish full circle round.'

7. Gaze at the candle (imagining it with a lit flame) for about a minute while you focus on your wish.
8. Leave the grid in place for one lunar cycle, and you will discover that loving your wish actually means you will be able to fulfil it too.

A Ritual to Embrace Change

Some of us thrive on change, while others resist it. Just like how drawing the Death card from a tarot deck can either fill us with irrational fear, or be seen as a symbol of much needed transformation. Working with the power of this card will help you not only enrich your life, but accept and use change to your benefit.

The card usually signifies the end of one cycle in life and the beginning of a new one, and if we look at the card in this way, we can face change with a fearless attitude and love it for what it is. Perhaps it is simply about decluttering or removing something obstructive? Or perhaps it requires a complete change of attitude? Whatever you want to change or are resistant to changing may be the pathway to a new self-loving you, so give it a try.

You will need:
a tarot deck
a white candle
a pink tourmaline crystal
2 pieces of citrine

1. Light the candle, and place the two pieces of citrine on either side of it.
2. Shuffle the deck of cards, as many times as you intuitively feel necessary, and then place them face down on the table.
3. Cut the deck three times, and then place the deck face down again.

4. Turn over the cards one by one, making a new face-up pile to the right until you come to the Death card. For a moment focus on it and then ask yourself the following questions:

- What change are you hoping for?
- What do you need to relinquish?
- What change is necessary to love yourself more?

5. If answers come to mind, write them down.
6. The card that comes after the Death card will indicate what you need to let go of, or what needs to be left behind. Place it above the Death card.
7. The card that came before the Death card will tell you what you now need to focus on to love yourself more. Place it beneath the Death card.
8. Call on your intuition to interpret these two cards and what they might mean in relation to your questions. Tarot interpretations can be easily found online or in any good book on tarot.

You need to realise that death isn't something to fear, but a symbol of change. It's time to wholeheartedly embrace change and be the best version of you.

Now that you are working with practices and rituals to develop and nurture self-esteem and self-awareness, you should begin to develop a better understanding and appreciation of who you truly are.

Chapter Three

Radiating Positivity

'Don't be satisfied with stories, how
things have gone with others. Unfold
your own myth.'

Rumi

Now that you've started learning how to love yourself,
flaws and all, you're ready to learn how to cultivate positivity in your life using the magical power of the planets.
In this chapter you will understand how to use your zodiac
sign to unlock your potential and discover the best possible
pathway for the future.

Self-Empowerment Rituals with the Planets

In order to cultivate positivity and open our hearts to love and happiness, we need to have the conviction and courage to live as our authentic selves, rather than by other people's expectations.

In Roman mythology, the seven planets (at the time Uranus, Neptune and Pluto had not been discovered) were identified with gods who embodied their energies. In astrology, these qualities are also assigned to the planets in your birth chart. In ancient Greece, these gods were the sun Helios, the moon Selene, Aphrodite, Hermes, Ares, Zeus, and Cronos. By working with the different planets, you will be empowered by their unique energies.

Sun Ritual for Shining Your Light

As Helios rides his chariot across the heavens by day, you too are going to spend a day of shining as brightly as the sun to discover how to celebrate your talents with integrity and self-belief. Loving yourself this way means you don't have to rely on anyone else to do the praising for you.

You will need:
a hand mirror
a handful of gold stars
a pouch

10 small pieces of citrine
a yellow candle

1. On a sunny morning, hold your hand mirror and turn it to reflect the sky and the sun for about 30 seconds without looking directly at the sun itself. As you do say: 'This mirror draws down the power of the sun to help me shine brightly in any way I choose.'
2. Without touching the mirror's reflective surface, leave it face down on a table for the rest of the day.
3. In the evening, go back to the table and light your yellow candle. Then take your pouch and fill it with the gold stars and citrine.
4. Repeat:

    'With golden stars and solar joy,
    I find myself enlightened now,
    Take candles, citrine, mirrored sun,
    To find my own self from now on.'

5. Place the pouch in front of the candle. Now pick up your mirror and gaze at your reflection. Imagine the sun god shining his beneficial light directly on you from the mirror, enhancing all your talents so that you can truly shine.

Repeat the above ritual whenever you need to boost your solar sparkle, and realise you are as dazzling as the sun itself.

MOON RITUAL TO CONNECT WITH YOUR FEELINGS

The moon symbolises our feelings, moods and emotions, and some believe it has a direct effect on them too. Like the goddess Selene, the moon is ambivalent, both loving but possessive. Selene fell in love with the Aeolian shepherd, Endymion, and kept him all for herself by asking Zeus to cast a spell of eternal sleep over him. Selene was also responsible for the changing tides and how they influenced life on Earth. Connect to her power to see that you have a right to the feelings and emotions of the moon's ways and can align to her cycles of ebb and flow, coming and going.

This ritual is best carried out on the evening of a new crescent moon.

You will need:
a symbol or image of a new crescent moon
a bunch of lavender
a bowl of water
4 moonstones
4 white tea-light candles

1. Begin by dropping the four moonstones into the bowl of water, before gently sprinkling on the lavender.
2. Then place a candle at each of the compass points to form a circle around your bowl. Light the

candles and for the next minute focus on the flickering flames, or their reflections in the water.

3. Then say:

'With water's soul and lunar spells
I charge my life with feeling's well,
And those that come that I resist
Are just as real as those I've blessed.
If love is here, I'll welcome more
To chase the serpent from the door,
Yet all who feel across this world
Connect by oceans in their soul.
With left of right and north of south,
I share this spell to take my right
For lunar love and loving care,
And by the tides I make this prayer.'

4. Stir the water round gently with your finger to seal your intention for caring for your feeling world. Leave the bowl in place until the full moon to activate your connection to the ebb and flow of lunar energy and acceptance of your changing moods.

VENUS RITUAL FOR SELF-WORTH AND TO REMOVE SELF-DOUBT

Aphrodite may have been vain, but she understood the importance of value. Whether it's material, emotional or intrinsic, having any kind of value in life means you can live with integrity and be free from doubt.

Here's a simple Venus ritual to align you to your own principles and to stand by them, especially when someone or something sows a seed of doubt in your mind. It will enable you to trust in your authentic truth.

You will need:
4 rose quartz crystals
4 bay leaves
4 x 1ft lengths of gold ribbon or cord, each with four equidistant knots
rose essential oil

1. Place your rose quartz crystals so they resemble the four petals of a flower. Place a bay leaf between each crystal.
2. Encircle your 'flower' with the four ribbons so that you have four concentric circles.
3. Focus on your flower for about 30 seconds. Then say:

    'My boundaries are firm and my heart is sure,
    I give thanks to Venus to bring me this cure.
    To value what's mine, safeguarded by herbs,
    To banish self-doubt, or belittling words.
    With rose quartz I'm bonded and true to myself,
    So blessed is this flower that fills me with worth.'

4. Drizzle the essential oil onto the four crystals. Take up each crystal in turn and gently stamp the back of your other hand with the oiled surface of each crystal to affirm your intention to give value to your integrity.

You will now be able to go out in the world without fear of being devalued by others, with stronger boundaries and belief in yourself.

MERCURY RITUAL FOR GOOD COMMUNICATION

Being truly self-empowered also relies on being able to communicate successfully. Hermes (Mercury's Greek counterpart) was the god of trade, magic, transition, crossroads and liminal places (thresholds). He was known for his ability to establish successful communication and beneficial commercial transactions and was revered at crossroads, as it was believed he would look favour-ably upon travellers or for those passing through to the underworld. This ritual will enable you to cross over any 'threshold', whether you're pitching ideas, trying to market yourself, or making yourself clear to someone, and get your message across.

You will need:
a doorway, entrance, porch
a bunch of basil

a pen and a piece of fairly thick (say 220gsm)
    paper, A4 size
a length of white ribbon
a length of black ribbon
a white tea-light candle

1. Choose your dedicated threshold, and light the candle nearby. Place or hang the bunch of basil under the threshold itself (if you can't hang it, place it on a step, directly beneath the arch or lintel of the doorway, but obviously somewhere it won't get trodden on!).
2. Before you begin to write on your paper, focus on what you need to communicate right now, and to whom? Then write your intention as clearly as possible.
3. Roll up the paper, and tie the two ribbons around it and secure with a bow.
4. Stand in one space or the other, but not in the actual threshold and say:

    'Hermes my guide, show me the way
    To speak my mind and make my day.
    For as I cross from edge to edge,
    All fears be gone and message read,
    And those who hear will be in praise
    Of all that's said, invoked, ablaze.'

5. Now pick up your scroll, and take one step into the middle of your threshold, and say: 'Once I

cross this threshold, my words will be invoked, understood and accepted.'

6. Now step into the other space, and place the scroll on the ground. Stand for a moment or so focused on your intention and the words you want to communicate, and thank Hermes for helping you to deliver your missive.

When the time comes to get your message across, it will be to your benefit.

MARS RITUAL FOR MANIFESTING A POSITIVE OUTCOME

The handsome, battle-lusting Ares was the Greek god of war. He is often remembered for his affair with Aphrodite, which came to an abrupt end after the lovers were discovered and humiliated by Aphrodite's husband, Hephaestus. Despite this though, Ares was strength personified: courageous, unstoppable, egocentric and carefree. He symbolises motivation, turning thoughts into action, and the power to accomplish great things. So harness this feisty Martian energy to manifest your goals.

You will need:
a red carnelian bracelet or twelve small red
   carnelian stones
a piece of paper and a pen
a red tea-light candle

1. Write down what it is you wish to manifest. This should be one thing you know is possible but which requires personal effort, imagination, self-belief or practical resources to get it off the ground.

2. Place your bracelet on the written statement or, if you're using carnelian stones, form a circle around it. Then place the unlit red candle in the middle of your bracelet or stone circle.

3. Now say:

    'With fiery power and powerful fire,
    My goal is fixed to my desire,
    These stones they circle all that's set,
    To manifest my true intent.'

4. Focus on the red candle for a minute or so and find stillness (you can imagine it lit and the flame flickering too). To seal your intention to manifest your goal, leave everything in place for twenty-four hours to invoke the blessings of Mars and channel his ability to get things done.

JUPITER RITUAL FOR LUCK AND OPPORTUNITY

Beneficial Jupiter is the Roman counterpart of the Greek god of the heavens, Zeus. Zeus was a promiscuous, charming, seductive opportunist with mortals, nymphs and goddesses alike and luck, it seems, was pretty much on his side. He was known for hurling thunder and light-ning bolts through the skies – he also seduced the mortal Semele, in the guise of a bolt of lightning, filling her with his fire.

This ritual will invoke this kind of positive, electrifying energy, bringing you good luck so that you can seize any opportunity, take a calculated risk, or orchestrate things so that you're in the right place at the right time.

You will need:
2 pieces of lapis lazuli
an image of lightning (or if it's a particularly stormy night, you can observe lightning from the safety of your home)

1. Face your chosen source of lightning while holding a piece of lapis in each hand (the lapis forms an invisible circuit of psychic protective energy – although it doesn't protect you against physical storms!).
2. Now say:

   'These stones they bring a lucky strike
   When blessed by Zeus throughout the night,
   By day they show the moment struck
   To find myself with lapis luck.'

3. Place the two pieces of lapis on a window ledge and leave in place for twenty-four hours to be charged with the luck of the god.

4. The next day, pick a piece of lapis to take with you as you go about your day – the other piece should be left in place for one lunar cycle. Be prepared for lucky opportunities to come your way.

SATURN RITUAL FOR DETERMINATION AND PERSEVERANCE

When you know what you truly want, whether that's a dream job, a change of lifestyle, a reward for your creativity or just to be truly loved for who you are (and that also includes honestly loving yourself too), this last ritual in this planet series will help you to persevere and achieve that aim.

Before Saturn became known as the Roman god of time, duty and obligation, his Greek predecessor was Cronus, the father of Zeus. The astrological Saturn reminds us how with determined effort we can achieve results, stand by our gut instincts and achieve success through self-discipline and perseverance. Acorns are symbolic of strength, longevity and endurance and are used in magic work to represent the diligence and mettle that Saturn describes in our birth charts.

This ritual is best carried out on the evening of a waxing moon.

You will need:
3 pieces of onyx or smoky quartz
3 acorns

3 red tea-light candles
sandalwood essential oil

1. Begin by placing the candles in a row in front of
    you, making sure that they're nicely spaced out.
    Then form a triangle in front of the central candle
    using your acorns. Take your three precious stones
    and form a second triangle that will sit behind the
    central candle. Once everything is in place, care-
    fully light your three candles.
2. Gaze into the candle flames for a minute and
    find stillness. Then, hold up each acorn in turn
    as you say:

    'With oak tree strength I find my need
    With leaves of earth I will achieve,
    My quest will never be undone
    'Til time is set and all is won.
    With Saturn's work the future's cast,
    For now I've strength to leave the past.'

3. Blow out the candles and complete this ritual by
    dropping a little of the sandalwood oil onto your
    three stones to set your intention to persevere to
    achieve your future goals.
4. Leave this grid in place until the full moon. Repeat
    during any waxing moon, or whenever you need
    to boost your determined spirit.

Vocational Rituals with the Zodiac

By embracing and acknowledging our hidden potential, we can learn to appreciate our talents and establish a stronger connection with our authentic self. But what are our hidden potentials? These are usually our talents or gifts that go unnoticed or remain locked away in our psyche due to the expectations imposed on us by family and friends, or the society in which we live. When we finally connect with our hidden gifts, it can feel like an epiphany that provides great clarity and direction.

It's common to believe that our sun sign (generally referred to as our star sign) only provides a sense of our characteristic traits, but it actually reveals our purpose in life, our sense of vocation and our life direction. When we take a few steps along a particular road associated with our sun sign, we can discover real meaning in life, along with a positive attitude to loving yourself and your future pathway.

Some of us are lucky enough to have found the way to our true calling, others follow careers according to what's expected of them, and many of us just wallow in meaningless jobs or flit from one thing to another, never really content with anything we do. But once you have a sense of that calling, that's when you start to feel true love for it too.

The first ritual will give you an idea of your current attitude towards your calling.

SENSE OF CALLING RITUAL

You will need:
a 1ft length of twine or white ribbon
a book
a smoky quartz crystal
an apple
4 white candles

1. Place the candles in a row in front of you and then place each item by a candle. Now light the candles.
2. Close your eyes, and slowly move your index finger to point at each candle in turn, scanning the row intuitively.
3. Move your finger back and forth for about thirty seconds or so, as you repeat: 'This light brings knowledge, these symbols will enlighten my way.'
4. Connect with your intuition and when you feel ready to stop moving your finger, open your eyes. Which item are you pointing at? Each of the four symbolises a different aspect of your potential that you may need to unlock.

- **The apple** (symbol of confidence, growth): you want the people around you to think highly of you and although you have talents you want to show off, you're too scared by the thought of failure to put yourself outside your comfort zone. By becoming more assertive, people are more likely to bite into your apple.

- **The book** (symbol of knowledge, communication): you're very proud of your skills, do things by the book and have utter belief in yourself. However, you need to learn to better listen to other people's advice, and have more communication with others so that you can encounter people who will help you discover your true pathway.
- **The crystal** (symbol of personal creativity, manifestation): you're open to anything new, as long as it allows you to remain independent. Being creative is one thing, but you may feel people demand too much of you and prefer not to commit yourself to anything. Learn to persevere a little and you'll achieve your creative goals.
- **The white ribbon** (symbol of independence): you like to feel the support of others around you, and rely on their praise as a source of motivation. Yet now is the time to become more self-reliant. You will succeed in anything if you trust in your intuition rather than other people's expectations.

This oracle has given you quick insight into your current state of being. When linked to the vocations and pathways associated with your sign, you can begin the search for your true calling.

ARIES
Ruling planet: Mars
Symbol: the Ram
Crystal: red carnelian

Best qualities: fiery, driven, challenging, courageous and energetic

Best suited to a career in: finance, politics, sports, emergency services, project management and travel

RITUAL FOR SETTING OFF ON THE RIGHT PATHWAY

You will need:
a white tea-light candle
a red tea-light candle

1. Light both of your candles and then carefully drop a little wax from the white candle onto the red and vice versa.
2. As you do so say:

   'I am this fire, and I am this flame,
   As strong as this Aries that lies in my name.
   With fabulous fire I will soon light my way,
   And the sparks they will lead me to my
   *   perfect day.'*

3.   Blow out the candles to seal your intention to the universe and to ensure that you will soon be skipping along the right road to vocational success.

TAURUS
Ruling planet: Venus
Symbol: the Bull
Crystal: emerald

Best qualities: creative, practical, stable, cautious, sensual and nature-loving

Best suited to a career in: landscape, interior or graphic design, creative arts, gardening, art restoration and antiques

RITUAL FOR SETTING OFF ON THE RIGHT PATHWAY

You will need:
a rough emerald

1.   Hold a piece of rough emerald in one hand, close your eyes and then raise it to your third eye chakra (midway between your eyebrows). Visualise a specific vocation as you say:

'With bravest heart and bullish soul,
I'll find my way down this new road,

And all my talents sure and sound,
Will bring a path that's now my own.'

2. Keep the stone in a safe place for one lunar cycle and you will be able to tread down your chosen path with ease, and delight at what you find there.

GEMINI
Ruling planet: Mercury
Symbol: the Twins
Crystal: citrine

Best qualities: entertaining, free-spirited, charming, versatile, witty and light-hearted

Best suited to a career in: journalism, bookselling, copywriting, languages, illustration and travel writing

RITUAL FOR SETTING OFF ON THE RIGHT PATHWAY

You will need:
a piece of citrine
frankincense essential oil

1. Place your citrine in a sunny spot, and drizzle a few drops of frankincense essential oil over it as you say:

    'With frankincense my quest's begun,

To find my path with citrine's sun,
My talents found, projects in view,
To set off now for pastures new.'

2.   Leave the stone for twenty-four hours to invoke
     your intention to set off on a new vocational path,
     and to bring you the luck you deserve.

CANCER
Ruling planet: the Moon
Symbol: the Crab
Crystal: moonstone

Best qualities: caring, gentle, sensitive, intuitive, sensual, nostalgic, psychic and creative

Best suited to a career in: social care, historical research, counselling, catering, nursing and midwifery, hotel and catering, and human resources

RITUAL FOR SETTING OFF ON
THE RIGHT PATHWAY

This ritual is best performed on the evening of a full moon.

You will need:
3 moonstones
a white candle

1. Place the white candle on a flat surface and form a triangle around it with your moonstones. Light the candle and say:

   'With careful thought I leave this hearth,
   To know my true way from my heart,
   With lunar love I'll feel the way,
   And find my calling from this day.'

2. Blow out the candle and leave the moonstones in place for one lunar cycle and you will begin to see the right pathway opening up before you.

LEO
Ruling planet: the Sun
Symbol: the Lion
Crystal: tiger's eye

Best qualities: dramatic, stylish, self-aware, fiery, romantic, glamorous and loving

Best suited to a career in: acting, film and entertainment, motivational speaking, event management, fashion design and restaurant management

RITUAL FOR SETTING OFF ON THE RIGHT PATHWAY

This ritual is best performed at sunset on a sunny day.

You will need:
a packet of sunflower seeds

1. Visit one of your favourite spots in nature and find a small patch of earth to scatter your sunflower seeds. The idea is to pick a place where the seeds might flourish, although it doesn't matter if they don't take root as it's the symbolic act of sowing these sunny seeds that matters. As you do so, say:

    'With sunflowers bright I turn my head,
    To see the road to make new threads,
    Of golden light and golden braids,
    Where I can still be centre stage.'

2. Your ritual is now sealed and you can begin to make exciting plans to fulfil your vocational destiny.

VIRGO
Ruling planet: Mercury
Symbol: the Virgin
Crystal: peridot

Best qualities: dedicated, selective, discerning, intellectual, precise, ordered and sensual

Best suited to a career in: publishing, nutrition, fitness and health, psychotherapy, accountancy and sustainable resources

RITUAL FOR SETTING OFF ON THE RIGHT PATHWAY

This ritual is best performed on the evening of a waxing moon.

You will need:
a book of your choosing
a pen
4 slips of paper

1. On each piece of paper write down one of the following words: 'Sense', 'Discerning', 'Vocation' and 'Reward'. Now open up your chosen book and place your slips of paper in it at random, and then leave everything in place until the next full moon.
2. When you return to your book, gently remove the slips of paper. Hold each corresponding piece of paper in your hand as you repeat the following verse:

   'Good "sense" I have to start my quest,
   "Discerning" insight brings the best,
   "Vocation" pathways I can find,
   "Rewarding" me with active time.'

3. You will soon be walking down the right pathway to your vocational dream.

LIBRA
Ruling planet: Venus
Symbol: the Scales
Crystal: sapphire

Best qualities: sophisticated, rational, idealistic, aesthetic, romantic, generous and seductive

Best suited to a career in: beauty, art, relationship therapy, fashion design and law

RITUAL FOR SETTING OFF ON THE RIGHT PATHWAY

This ritual is performed on the evening of a full moon.

You will need:
5 pieces of red carnelian

1. Before you start this ritual, ensure that you have a large, clear indoor or outdoor space to work from. You will need to ensure that the grid you are about to create will be undisturbed for an entire lunar cycle.
2. Create a pentagram using your red carnelian – it should be big enough for you to stand comfortably

in the centre. Once you're in position, turn to face each crystal, moving anti-clockwise, and repeat the following as you do so:

'My love for self is growing strong,
I know my way now, all be done.
My pathway's heart I will achieve,
And bless my world creatively.'

3. Leave your pentagram in place for one lunar cycle. Then, when the time comes, step into the centre again and repeat the above magic verse. You can now gather up your red carnelian and store them in a safe space. Watch as your chosen career path lights up before you.

SCORPIO
Ruling planet: Pluto
Symbol: the Scorpion
Crystal: obsidian

Best qualities: passionate, mysterious, intense, self-contained, powerful, serious and shrewd

Best suited to a career in: police and security services, criminology, hypnotherapy or sex therapy, financial services and forensic science

RITUAL FOR SETTING OFF ON THE RIGHT PATHWAY

This ritual is best performed during a new crescent moon phase.

You will need:
4 small black crystals or stones of your choice

1. Find a quiet open space to carry out this ritual — ideally this would be somewhere that you can easily visit whenever you're in need of inspiration. Then take your four stones and bury them at the base of a tree, bush or large shrub of your choice. Repeat the following charm as you do so:

    'With darkest stones my light is found,
    I place these crystals in the ground,
    My future pathway's set and clear,
    And all desire be unearthed here.'

2. By the next new moon you will be able to enjoy newfound clarity when it comes to your career.

SAGITTARIUS
Ruling planet: Jupiter
Symbol: the Archer
Crystal: turquoise

Best qualities: optimistic, high-spirited, free-spirited, generous and romantic

Best suited to a career in: travel, teaching, photography, politics, entertainment and ecology

RITUAL FOR SETTING OFF ON THE RIGHT PATHWAY

You will need:
an image of a place that you would like to visit
a piece of turquoise
a blue tea-light candle

1. Begin by placing the turquoise on your image. Then place your candle directly in front of you and light it.
2. Now say:

    'Enchanting places, other times,
    I'll find my way without these rhymes,
    Yet all that's in my future bright,
    Accomplished spirit, now in sight.'

3. Blow out the candle and keep the turquoise with you for one lunar cycle to establish your new career journey.

CAPRICORN
Ruling planet: Saturn

Symbol: the Sea-Goat
Crystal: ruby

Best qualities: ambitious, loyal, self-reliant, confident, realistic and accomplished

Best suited to a career in: property development and management, film and entertainment, museum curator and sales

RITUAL FOR SETTING OFF ON THE RIGHT PATHWAY

This ritual is best performed at sunset.

You will need:
4 red tea-light candles
4 pieces of serpentine (malachite also works well if
   you're finding serpentine difficult to source)
a rough ruby

1. As the sun sets, form an alternating circle of serpentine and red candles. Then place your ruby in the centre of this circle. Then repeat:

    'With ruby red and green desire,
    I make my future and aspire
    To greater things, ambitions set,
    A "fait accompli", no regrets.'

2. Blow out the candles, but leave your formation in place until the next day. In the weeks to come you will discover a new direction that calls to you and will bring you success.

AQUARIUS
Ruling planet: Uranus
Symbol: the Water-Bearer
Crystal: amber

Best qualities: avant-garde, intellectual, glamorous, independent and compassionate

Best suited to a career in: social media, humanitarian reform, animal rights and environmental sciences

RITUAL FOR SETTING OFF ON THE RIGHT PATHWAY

You will need:
3 x 2ft lengths of gold twine or cord

1. Begin by knotting together the ends of your three lengths of twine and then make a further knot in the middle, so that you have three knots. Repeat the following as you hold each of your three knots:

    'This knotted three, brings pathways new,
    Where fresh ideas will conjure views

Of insight, change and future dreams,
And all the world will love my schemes.'

2. Keep the knotted charm in an envelope and write your intended vocational direction on the outside. Keep in a safe place for one lunar cycle to realise your career intention.

PISCES
Ruling planet: Neptune
Symbol: the Fish
Crystal: amethyst

Best qualities: imaginative, artistic, creative, caring and versatile

Best suited to a career in: alternative therapies, working with animals, social care and creative industries

RITUAL FOR SETTING OFF ON THE RIGHT PATHWAY

This ritual is best performed on the evening of a new crescent moon.

You will need:
a needle
a candle

1. With the needle, carve one word that sums up your aspirations for your career on the side of a candle. Then light the candle and wait for it to burn down into the word you've engraved, before blowing it out to seal your intention to the universe. Then say:

   'With wishes made I'm true to self,
   Here light the flame for inner wealth.
   Give to myself the pathway clear,
   So I can follow all that's dear.'

2. Light the candle again at the full moon, and repeat the incantation to reinforce your wish to be realised by the next full moon.

Now that you understand your personal talents and vocational desires, you can begin to express and manifest them. Once you start loving the unique talents that make you feel good to be you, then that kind of self-care will boost your confidence, bring you a realisation of self-acceptance and an understanding of who you really are and who you are becoming.

So now, with your intentions set in motion, and with a revival of love in your authentic self, take time to love the sensual you too.

Chapter Four

Loving the Sensual You

'Through and through me
Beneath the flesh
Impalpable fire runs tingling.'

Sappho

Loving yourself is also about nourishing and caring for your sensuality – your senses – and this chapter will offer magical ways to connect to and hone them. The rituals here will allow you to feel completely in sync with your body and encourage you to develop a new appreciation for it too.

We don't often think about our 'sensual health' in the same way that we do our mental and physical wellbeing – but our senses are integral to how we experience the world. From breathing in the heady scent of a flower, to listening to a chorus of birdsong and taking a scenic walk, to observing a breath-taking sunset, our sensuality defines how we interact with the natural world. This chapter will encourage you to cultivate sensual awareness so that you can be more present, engaged and fulfilled.

This first practice will awaken you to your physical needs, and enable you to delight in your sensual self.

The Goddess in You

In magic, we call on mythological goddesses to embody certain archetypes or qualities intrinsic to us all. This ritual will help you to honour your feminine mystique by reconnecting to this wisdom, so you can truly love and nurture the sensual you.

The quiz below will allow you to discover the goddess energy that is most active in your life right now, so that you can focus on your current sensual needs. Once you've discovered which goddess you are aligned with, you can engage with the corresponding ritual to balance and bring awareness to what you might need to work on. Your goddess energy may change from time to time, depending on your life experiences, so you can come back to this quiz as often as you like.

Note down your answers to each of the following questions and see whether you have mostly a, b, c or d.

1. What best sums up your attitude towards your sensuality right now?
a) I indulge freely in all my senses.
b) I love pampering myself and being seductive.
c) I'm not too bothered if my needs aren't met.
d) My sensuality is sacred, so I find it hard to let anyone in.

2. How would you ask your partner for a hug?
a) I'd ask outright.
b) We're always hugging – there's no need to ask.
c) I'd drop subtle hints that I hope they'd pick up on.
d) They should know instinctively when I need a hug.

3. How would you react if your partner doesn't want a hug?
a) It's not the end of the world, sometimes you want your personal space.
b) Laugh and throw them on the bed.
c) I never ask, so I wouldn't know.
d) I would feel vulnerable and hurt.

5. How do you rate your sensual confidence?
a) When I'm flirting with someone I'm interested in, it's ten out of ten.
b) Although I'm good at appearing confident when I'm with someone I like, sometimes it's just a front.

c) Generally low, but it improves once I get to know someone better.

d) It's good, but only when I'm the dominant partner.

6. If your partner isn't meeting your sexual needs, what do you do?

a) Have an open and honest conversation with my partner.

b) It's time to get into seductive mode and try new things.

c) Nothing. It's safer.

d) Let resentment fester or decide it's time to find a new partner.

How did you score? You may find that you have a balance of two or three energies, in which case work on what feels instinctively most pressing to you first.

Mostly a – Aphrodite: seductively aware of physical charm.

Mostly b – Calypso: romantic, 'in love' with love.

Mostly c – Hestia: cool and detached about sensuality.

Mostly d – Lilith: deeply sensual, acutely vulnerable.

APHRODITE

Vain but beautiful Aphrodite was the embodiment of female wisdom and sexual power. She would restore youth and beauty to those who worshipped her. In Greek myth she was married off to the undesirable Hephaestus, yet she rarely shared his bed. Her lovers included Ares, the potent god of war, and Adonis, whom she eventually had to share with Persephone.

YOUR STRENGTHS

Aphrodite types know exactly how to seduce and turn their lovers on. Confident and caring, you also know that it's essential for you to have some space and time to yourself. You're sexually creative, sensually indulgent and exciting to be with.

WHAT YOU NEED TO DEVELOP

Aphrodite types are very aware of their seductive nature, their beauty and sensuality. Learn that true self-esteem comes from within rather than from how well you performed in bed or what you look like. Aphrodite types are often drawn to relationships where they can feel in control, so you need to let go of the reins a little and let your partner take time to get to know you.

AFFIRMATION

My sensual purpose is to develop trust in myself and others.

TRUST RITUAL

This ritual is best performed on a windy day.

You will need:
a handful of rose petals
lavender essential oil

Choose a scenic, outdoor area to scatter your rose petals. Follow them as they're carried along by the wind and once they have settled on the ground, take a step back to see which petals instinctively catch your eye. Home in on one petal in particular, whichever one speaks to you, and drip some of your lavender oil on to this petal. Take this sacred petal and keep it with you for the rest of the day to inspirit you with trust, love and self-awareness.

CALYPSO

The gentle enchantress Calypso lived on the beautiful island of Ogygia. When she found the hero Odysseus washed up on her beach, she fell in love with him at first sight and he stayed on her island for seven years. The couple had two sons, Nausinous and Nausithous, and by most accounts Calypso and Odysseus were very much in love and happy with one another. But when the Olympian gods intervened to command Odysseus to return home, the self-sacrificing Calypso reluctantly helped her lover build a raft. When it came to set sail, Odysseus delayed his departure, choosing to stay one more day with his beloved Calypso.

YOUR STRENGTHS

Enchanting and charming, you're an utter romantic and will always put your partner first. You fall in love quickly and give your all to your relationships. Delighting in the joy of life, your partner is mesmerised by your fun-loving spirit and gentle soul.

WHAT YOU NEED TO DEVELOP

Calypsos need to learn to take as well as give. You're prone to committing too quickly to relationships where you're shouldering the majority of the emotional labour. Try not to let your relationship define your sense of self-worth. Are you in a relationship because you want to prove you're worthy of love, or do you want a partner with whom you can share the good times and the bad? It's time to discover what you truly need and deserve from a relationship.

AFFIRMATION

I must honour my right to take as well as give.

SELF-AWARENESS RITUAL

You will need:
cypress essential oil
2 seashells
samphire
seaweed

1. Begin by finding a quiet outdoor spot – this could be your garden, or somewhere along a favourite scenic walk. Drizzle a little of the cypress essential oil on the two seashells, then gently place them in an unobtrusive spot. Say:

   'Calypso loves from enchanted isles
   Her sensual self it knows all wiles,

> *But I'll never lead myself astray*
> *Nor let romance take me away.'*

2. Cover your petition to Calypso with a little sam-
    phire and seaweed, making sure that both shells
    are fully covered. You will soon be able to express
    your true sensual needs more freely.

HESTIA

The Greek goddess of the home and hearth, Hestia was
gentle, modest and self-possessed. The sister of Zeus, she
played a passive role among the soap-opera-like antics of
her siblings. Her power was like that of the eternal flame
of the hearth. Constant and true, Hestia's fire in Greek
households was never allowed to go out.

YOUR STRENGTHS

Easy-going and conflict-adverse, Hestias delight in a warm
sensual embrace and enjoy letting their partner take the
lead. Loving and kind, you respect your partner's sexual
needs and put their desires first. Long-term commitment
is an important consideration for you in every relationship.

WHAT YOU NEED TO DEVELOP

If you identify with Hestia, you must learn to be assertive
about your needs, even if you think you don't have any.
You do. It is time to venture forth, liberate yourself from
the constraints of your mind and the narrow view you
have of your sensuality.

AFFIRMATION
I will devote myself to being more frank and spontaneous about my desires.

ASSERTING MYSELF RITUAL

This ritual is best carried out on the night of a full moon.

You will need:
6 red tea-light candles
a piece of red carnelia

1. Find a suitable flat surface, and form a circle around the red carnelian with your candles. Then light each candle in turn. Repeat:

   'These stones of red they open my eyes,
   It's time now to tell all that's good and wise.
   My senses alight with my passions untamed
   I'll never be fearful of lighting my flame.'

2. Leave your petition to Hestia in place overnight, and you will find you can be more honest about your need for warmth and sensual closeness.

LILITH
Lilith was handmaiden to the Sumerian goddess Innana. She acted as a guide to Innana's temple, where people could enjoy sacred sexual rites. Lilith was debased by

patriarchal civilisations over the centuries and has been misrepresented as both a demon and a femme fatale. More recently, Lilith's original beauty has been re-established as a powerful archetype of sexual healing.

Your strengths
Potent and powerful, Liliths are free-spirited and rarely embarrassed about their sexual needs once in a mutually exclusive partnership. You love indulging in erotic or intensely passionate sex and will usually be the dominant partner.

What you need to develop
Liliths must learn to surrender to the deepest power that lies within, that of integrity and emotional honesty. Although you're a very private person, sometimes you're willing to give your all to a passionate love affair, as the relationship can act as a mask for your own vulnerability. Liliths might also experience jealousy or push their partners away due to a fear of rejection. Be more open about your desires and honour the Lilith within.

Affirmation
I acknowledge my instinctive passion and express my pleasure without pretence.

EMOTIONAL HONESTY RITUAL

You will need:
a small goblet, cup or glass
rose water
a garnet or piece of red jasper
a red tea-light candle

1. Fill the goblet with the rose water and then light the candle. Say: 'With Lilith's healing power and strength, I will show desire without pretence.'
2. Place your crystal in the rose water and leave it there overnight. When you come to remove it in the morning, it will have been charged with Lilith's healing energy. Keep it close to you to encourage emotional honesty about your sexual needs.

ENCHANTMENT FOR CHARISMA

Charisma is one of those qualities that we tend to notice in other people. We all have someone who comes immediately to mind when we think of charisma. They walk into a room and everyone takes notice – somehow they seem to exude their own magic. Charisma is an ancient Greek word, meaning 'divine grace' and 'gift from the gods', and as such, is linked to the three Graces who were the attendants of Aphrodite. This gift of radiating beauty, elegance and happiness is within us all, so to exude charisma, perform the following enchantment.

This enchantment is best performed on the evening of a new moon.

You will need:
a white candle
a mirror
a piece of citrine
a piece of rose quartz
a piece of clear quartz

1. Place the candle in front of the mirror and light it. Then hold the citrine in front of your eyes and gaze beyond the crystal, focusing instead on your reflection in the mirror. As you do so, say: 'This citrine glows with dazzling gold, to give me power, charisma bold.'
2. Next hold up the rose quartz and say: 'This crystal brings me confidence, and beauty's child called elegance.'
3. Next hold up the clear quartz and say: 'This quartz aligns the Graces three, within my soul, to shine from me.'
4. The crystals have now been blessed with the energy of the Graces. Take the crystals with you whenever you want to radiate charisma, and feel connected to this gracious beauty within you.

Banishing Negative Energy

To love ourselves, we also need to clear the negative energies from the outside world that cling to us like dust and debris. This can be in the form of the negative psychic energy from the people around us, or from the geopathic stress linked to our environment. When we have such energies projected on to us, it's hard to see our own real, polished, dazzling self. We may even hide behind these dusty defences, not daring to be true to our own nature, fearful that shaking off such psychic debris might actually make us exposed or vulnerable.

So to love your actual physical body and its subtle energies, use this simple spring-cleaning practice to feel restored, cleansed and lovable. Finish off with a protective ritual to keep you psychically and physically safeguarded.

Personal Spring-Clean

To perform this ritual, you will need to find a pollution-free outdoor space – perhaps somewhere in the countryside or the seaside on a sunny day.

You will need:
a bottle of mineral water
a clear quartz crystal

1. Find a quiet, calm place to sit and gaze for a few moments at the lush landscape before you. Hold the quartz crystal in your hands close to your third eye chakra (midway between your eyes) and say: 'With this positive energy I cleanse my mind of all negativity.'

2. Now hold it to your throat chakra (close to your Adam's apple) and say: 'With this crystal I am cleansed of all intrusive negativity from others.'

3. Now hold the crystal to your heart chakra (mid chest) and say: 'With this crystal's connection to nature I am purified of all bad feelings.'

4. Now hold the crystal at your solar plexus chakra (upper belly) and say: 'My personal self is free from all bad influences.'

5. Hold the crystal to your sacral chakra (below your belly button) and say: 'I am cleansed of all psychic debris and dust.'

6. Finally, hold the crystal close to your base chakra (lower spine) and say: 'I am balanced and rooted to the earth, loved and held by its gentle powers, protected from its stresses and free from all negativity.'

7. When you have finished this little ritual, consecrate the crystal by pouring the mineral water over it.

8. You are now cleansed of psychic debris, protected from negativity, and you're ready to move through the world at ease.

Nurture Your Physical Magic

You may take up less physical space compared to an oak tree or an elephant, and more than a daisy or an ant, but your place in the universe isn't just a scientific measurement – it's a mystical one. To nurture and love your 'magical space' in the world, this ritual will invoke a sense of being part of the whole.

Perform this enchantment during the evening of a full moon.

You will need:

a rose
an image of a constellation of stars
a mirror
2 white candles

1. Place the rose and the image of the constellation before the mirror, and then place the two candles on either side and carefully light them.
2. Focus and find stillness by gazing into the candle flames in the mirror for a few minutes. Then make a circle with your hand by pressing together your forefinger and thumb. Imagine that it's a loupe and hold it nearer and nearer to the rose so that the flower fills as much of the circle as possible. Now, repeat the same step for the constellation.
3. Finally, hold your magical loupe up to your own reflection in the mirror until it frames your face. Say:

> *'In magic worlds nothing's sure,*
> *As every space takes less or more,*
> *So stars may shine as large or small,*
> *As flowers or faces in the glass.'*

4. Repeat this at every full moon to remind your-
    self of your true physical and psychic space in
    the universe.

WITCHING HOUR BATH ENCHANTMENT

We all need to take a break from our busy lives and enjoy
a true 'witching hour', when we can relax and restore our
outer and inner beauty. This bath-time ritual offers exactly
the breathing room you need.

This special bath enchantment is best performed on the
evening of a new crescent moon.

You will need:
4 red tea-light candles
4 pieces of amber
a handful of fresh lavender flowers
a handful of fresh mint
a handful of fresh rose petals
a favourite drink of your choice

1. Run a bath and add whatever fragrance, oil or bub-
    bles you personally prefer. Place a candle at each

corner of the bath, along with a piece of amber, before carefully lighting the candles.

2. Scatter your fresh herbs and flowers into the water as you say:

'My witching hour is timely now,
Restores my magic, invokes my power,
Where all my beauty shows delight,
And with this amber seals my night.'

3. Luxuriate in the bath for as long as you want — perhaps listen to a favourite playlist while sipping on your favourite drink. When you feel thoroughly relaxed, blow out the candles carefully. Choose a piece of amber and place it into the water to charge the stone with the water's sensual delights.

4. Keep the empowered amber beside your bed to restore and revive physical beauty as you sleep.

EMBRACE YOUR INNER BEAUTY RITUAL

Our inner beauty, that magical, numinous energy that radiates from us a bit like our charisma, is a force that can be hard to fathom. Yet here is a way to allow it to radiate more brightly, and to feel this energy flowing all around you. Time to unleash your inner 'beauty box' and welcome it into your life.

This hidden place resonates with one ancient myth concerning Psyche and Eros. When Aphrodite's son

Eros fell in love with the mortal Princess Psyche, who was thought to be even more beautiful than the goddess of love herself, Aphrodite became enraged. Fuelled by her anger, she set Psyche four seemingly impossible tasks, with the last requiring Psyche to descend into the underworld to capture some of Persephone's beauty in a small box. Although Psyche managed to fulfil the arduous task and return to the human world, she could not overcome her curiosity and peeked into the box instead of delivering it directly to Aphrodite – but the only thing inside was the essence of death. Psyche perished at once. Zeus, however, took pity on her by making her immortal and reuniting her with Eros. She became the personification of 'soul', depicted in ancient Greek iconography as a butterfly.

Similarly, there is an inner 'beauty box' hidden away in the depths of you, but this box is yours to open and will allow you to radiate your unique beauty.

This ritual is best performed on the evening of a waning moon (yes, waning as you are releasing energy from deep within you).

You will need:
a box
4 moonstones
4 dried pomegranate seeds

1. Begin by placing the four seeds in a row and form a second row beneath them with the moonstones.

2. Say:

> *'With north, south, east and west of me,*
> *With stones and seeds my beauty's freed,*
> *From hidden depths of treasures deep*
> *That bring to light my pure mystique.*
> *Moonstones release my love of self,*
> *For that's the beauty of this wealth;*
> *Pomegranates free my soul,*
> *For that's the beauty I unfold;*
> *Now with the spell my magic's cast*
> *And all around me love's held fast.'*

3. Place the stones and pomegranate seeds in the box until the new crescent moon, then take out into the countryside or your garden and freely scatter both stones and seeds to liberate your 'inner beauty' into the outer world.

Love Your Senses Rituals

We take our five senses – taste, touch, sight, sound and smell – for granted, but if you don't nurture them you begin to lose touch with the world around you. Here's how to re-establish your connection to nature by working with the four elements of astrological magic.

WATER RITUAL

The element of Water is associated with our feelings, not only emotional but also how we reach out to touch and feel the world around us. Touch is one of the most visceral and evocative senses. Our skin is highly sensitive and relays vibrations, signals and reactions via the nervous system to help us make sense of our surroundings. To help supercharge your sense of touch, you can perform this water ritual.

You will need:
a bowl of spring water

1. Sit beside your bowl of water and close your eyes. Gently lower your forefinger until it grazes the surface of the water, but don't let it sink beneath the surface. Let your finger rest upon the water for a moment and enjoy the sensation of the cool water against your skin. How would you describe this feeling?
2. This simple practice can be carried out in nature too. Over the next couple of days try to connect to your surroundings through touch, be it a blade of grass or the bark of a tree. Being more mindful of these experiences puts you in touch with your sense of being in the world.

EARTH RITUAL

Our senses of taste and smell, closely connected via our olfactory system, are informed by the element of Earth. Here's how to care for and be more aware of these two senses.

You will need:
a berry of your choice
a scented flower of your choice

1. Place the berry and the flower on a table. Then close your eyes and hold the flower to your nose, breathe in the fragrance until you become so accustomed to it that its smell starts to fade. Next pick up the berry and take a small bite of it, savouring the flavour. Now imagine it is ephemeral, passing and kissing your taste buds in the same way the perfumed flower kissed your nose. Imagine engaging in the smell and the taste of the flower and the berry at the same moment, what would that be like?
2. Now, do exactly that; hold the flower to your nose again as you take another bite of the berry. Can you separate the two sensations or have they merged to form one sensual experience?

This exercise will open you up to how these two senses are connected, but how differently we experience each in isolation. Loving these two senses will allow you to appreciate the beauty of the world around you.

AIR RITUAL

The element of Air is identified with language, voice, speech, communication and the sounds we hear. In folklore and magic, there is a belief that sound only exists if there is an ear to hear it. So open your ears to the sounds of nature, and you'll be surprised how you hear more in the world than you imagine. Out of sight is not always out of mind – especially if we hone our hearing, our most underused sense.

Begin this ritual in a peaceful outdoor space. Close your eyes and tune in to the sounds around you as you relax. At first you may just notice a general hum of activity, but as you concentrate, you'll be able to pick out individual sounds from birdsong to the rustle of leaves, and the whistling breeze to a cow lowing in the distance. The key is to realise there's so much going on around us that we automatically filter out on a daily basis.

This ritual will make you appreciate the rich symphony of the natural world that you may have unconsciously ignored.

FIRE RITUAL

Fire symbolises vision, dreams, illusions and our perspective on the world as we look through the lens of both our mind and our eyes. Our sense of sight is probably the one we trust the most. We see a face, read words on the page, like you are doing now, and think we know what we see is the truth – or at the very least, we recognise it for what it is. But can you see beyond what is there? Can you see through the apparent reality before you? Can you read between the lines and observe the real magic?

Try this ritual out to discover a new way of 'seeing' to discover a new dimension of your inherent magic.

You will need:
2 white candles

1. Light the two candles and watch each of the flames flicker and burn for about twenty seconds each until you are still and relaxed.
2. Now look beyond the flames and let your eyes focus on something in the distance, all the while still being aware of the flames before you.
3. Switch your gaze and focus on the flames again, but be more conscious of what's in your peripheral vision.
4. Finally, blow out the flames, and you may see wisps of colour as the candles begin to smoke. As you gaze around you, you will begin to see differently, not with your eyes, but with your sixth sense, the one that is coming to light through the other five.

Your Sixth Sense

Whether we call it our intuition, our sixth sense, or psychic awareness, this sense is one that each of us can enhance.

Practise this visualisation technique during every full moon to enhance awareness of your sixth sense. This visualisation takes you into a personal 'sanctuary', protecting you from the swirling psychic energies of others around you – and even your own overthinking mind.

The Sanctuary Visualisation

Close your eyes and visualise a beautiful view of the sea. You are standing at a very special high point, looking down on the ocean and beach below, with the horizon far in the distance. This is your own private look-out post that allows you to admire the wide expanse of the ocean. Here you are safe from rogue thoughts, the noisy messiness of daily life, and the negative chatter of the people around you.

Find a comfortable nook where you can rest in your sanctuary, sit there for a while and imagine the ocean before you, as you say: 'I am now in this high place, where I can be safe from psychic negativity and other energies. Here, I connect to my intuitive sense, and see the truth before me.'

Come out of your visualisation and whenever you have a gut feeling, or an intuitive moment, realise that it comes from this special protected place deep within you.

Your sixth sense is usually right, so work with it.

Love Your Chakras

One of the keys to holistic wellbeing is to care for and love our chakras. In Eastern traditions, these are invisible energy centres that are likened to spinning wheel gateways or sacred channels between the intrinsic energy of our human body and the flow of universal energy. So keeping these chakra gateways in good shape (I liken this to sweeping away the debris from dusty doorways) means we are more balanced and can allow beneficial energy to flow freely through us.

The following rituals are performed throughout the moon cycle to maximise the lunar energy associated with each chakra. They focus on one chakra at a time, but can be repeated whenever you would like to enhance their specific qualities.

CROWN CHAKRA

LOCATED
Crown of the head

ENERGY
Spiritual connection

Perform this ritual every new crescent moon to enhance connection to your spiritual self.

You will need:
2 clear quartz crystals

1. Stand facing in the direction of the sun. Hold the two clear quartz crystals, one in each hand, and say: 'I am clear and connected to the divine light which shines within me.'

2. Then raise both hands above your head in prayer pose and say: 'Blessed by the universe I am part of all and all is part of me.' Let your arms relax back to your sides and open your eyes. If you repeat this every new moon, you will soon feel animated with spiritual goodness.

THIRD EYE CHAKRA

LOCATED
Midway between the eyebrows

ENERGY
Intellect, intuition and psychic sense

Perform this ritual every waxing moon phase to vitalise and love your third eye chakra.

You will need:
a piece of lapis lazuli

1. Sit cross-legged with your back straight and your wrists resting on your knees.
2. Place the piece of lapis lazuli between your crossed legs.
3. Close your eyes and relax, and then say:

'With darkest lapis here I see
Beyond eyes bright for insight be,
My mind is filled with psychic power,
And all I know is truth that's found.'

4. Take the lapis lazuli and hold it between your eyebrows for ten seconds to connect to your psychic sense.
5. Repeat this ritual whenever you need to trust in your intuitive powers.

THROAT CHAKRA
LOCATED
Throat and neck

ENERGY
Communication

Perform this ritual every waxing moon to energise and balance your communicative powers.

You will need:
2 pieces of citrine
a yoga mat

1. Lie flat on your back on your yoga mat with your arms by your side.
2. Place the two pieces of citrine either side of your neck so they are just touching your skin.
3. Close your eyes and relax for a minute.

4. Imagine the golden light of the crystals infusing you with their magic to give you the communicative skills you need to get your message across, or the courage to say what's on your mind.
5. Come out of your little visualisation, gradually sit up, and thank the crystals for balancing your throat chakra.

HEART CHAKRA

LOCATED
Middle of upper chest

ENERGY
Love of self and others

You can do this ritual at any time between the new crescent moon and the full moon, but it's best done as near to the full moon as possible to maximise this heartfelt energy.

You will need:
a piece of rose quartz

1. Sit in a cross-legged position with your back straight.
2. Hold the piece of rose quartz close to your chest, and imagine the warmth of love radiating all around and through you.
3. Imagine the colour of the crystal unfurling through your aura, as it flows outwards to everyone and everything on this planet.

4. Say: 'This love is freely given to all of the universe, and I welcome love with my heart to fill me with joy, compassion and kindness.'
5. Continue to hold the crystal to your chest for another minute while you are mindful of the energy of love spreading through you.

SOLAR PLEXUS CHAKRA
LOCATED
Above the belly button

ENERGY
State of one's ego

This ritual is best performed on a full moon evening to empower and strengthen your ego.

1. To polish your ego without becoming arrogant, stand tall, then raise your right leg and rest the sole of your foot on your left thigh (the Tree pose in yoga).
2. Hold this pose for about twenty seconds, with hands in prayer before your chest. Then switch so that your left foot is resting on right thigh.
3. Stand tall and firm again on both legs and say, 'My ego is as strong as this tree, as solid and determined as my pose, yet I will never become arrogant or too proud, always gracious and respectful of other people's egos too.'

SACRAL CHAKRA

LOCATED
Lower belly

ENERGY
Sexuality and feelings

This ritual is best performed during a waning moon to promote sexual vitality and emotional strength.

You will need:
2 pieces of red carnelian
a yoga mat

1. Lie on your back on a yoga mat and hold a crystal in each hand. Then place one hand on your lower belly and the other to your heart.
2. Close your eyes and relax for about a minute to create a circuit of beneficial energy that flows through you.
3. Then say: 'With these red stones I heal and bring life to my sexual feelings, to nurture and love them, to express them and to honour them.'
4. Stay in this position for another minute or so and you will feel the energy radiating from the stones in your hands, blessing you with positive healing energy.

BASE OR ROOT CHAKRA
LOCATED
Base of spine

ENERGY
How grounded we are; our basic survival instinct

Perform only at the dark of the moon phase when the moon is not visible at all. This ritual will bring you a deep sense of how you we are intrinsically part of the cosmos, and therefore safe within it.

1. Stand outside in the darkness and raise your arms to the night sky. Feel your feet connected to the Earth, as if you have roots growing downwards like a tree. Sense the connection between you and the planet beneath you, and the link to the dark infinity above you as you reach out into the blackness. Sense a golden thread connecting you to the infinite nature of the universe.

Now that you have begun to enjoy and experience a greater sense of self-love, the next chapter will lead you through the tangled woods of personal love relationships, and how to navigate them.

PART TWO

Love of Others

'Love does not consist of gazing at
each other, but in looking together in
the same direction.'

Antoine de Saint-Exupery

Relationships can take many forms. You may find what began as an easy, no-strings-attached fling can blossom into a committed, long-term relationship; perhaps you become involuntarily entangled in a love triangle, or maybe you develop feelings for an old friend. The point is that it's not love that makes a relationship complicated, but the people in it.

When the magical force of love manifests in a relationship it can be a rush of emotions and contradictions, at once wild, unforgettable, kind, unforgiving, intuitive, ruthless, inspiring – and probably many other beautiful and painful things. Love leads us on journeys we never thought we might take, some are enticing, passionate, fulfilling, bonding and healing; others can be destructive, possessive, intense and tragic. Through love we learn about all the different sides of ourselves that we might never have known existed – and from each relationship, we understand what we need more and less of in the future.

As we've seen already, in ancient civilisations love was often personified as a deity. In the Western traditions of romantic and erotic love, it is most often embodied by Aphrodite and later her son Eros, who became Cupid of classical myth and who remains an iconic symbol of falling in love in Western art.

Falling In

One of the most mysterious forms of love is that of passionate desire. When we fall in love with someone – I'm talking about that head-over-heels, physically besotted, sexually mesmerised kind of feeling – we seem to be possessed *by* our emotions, rather than being in possession *of* them. This mysterious, spellbinding passion can strike at any time, but mostly when we feel an innate attraction to someone we can project our ideals onto – or who we believe to have some qualities that we lack. This kind of relationship is thought to be the psyche's way of reclaiming or owning a part of oneself that we apparently project onto the other. If we are able to separate ourselves from our subjectivity, we begin to realise that we are simply falling in love with our self.

Falling Apart or Together

Falling in love with someone whose qualities are actually hidden potentials within ourselves is known as love's mirroring effect. It might sound good on paper, but this kind of love can overwhelm and totally consume us. This level of intensity in a relationship is difficult to sustain long-term, and it's just as easy to fall apart as to fall in love if there is nothing to sustain that initial irrepressible attraction. This is where a relationship can either fizzle out, or evolve and develop into a long-term commitment with friendship, compromise, care and support.

This part of the book will provide you with rituals and spells for understanding and working with love and how it can weave in and out of our relationships. Chapter Five focuses on romantic and passionate love, Chapter Six on long-term commitment and loyalty, and finally Chapter Seven offers rituals and practices for loving family, friends and our home.

Chapter Five

Inviting Romance into Your Life

'You have witchcraft in your lips.'

Henry V, William Shakespeare

Ancient magical texts from around the world are filled with spells to find romance, to attract and manifest love into your life, and to encourage feelings to blossom in someone else's heart.

I cannot stress enough that the enchantments in this book are not designed to allow you to control or manipulate others – that would be a terrible thing to do! Instead, they should encourage romance, and perhaps long-term commitment, to blossom in your life. There are also rituals to awaken love in anyone who often struggles to accept it from others, or finds the idea of commitment frankly a little scary. If you truly believe in the magic you're creating and use it to send out positive energy to everyone around you, then the universe will thank you in return and help you to fulfil your deepest desires and nurture your soul.

Belief is everything in magic; without it, our wishes and intentions will stumble in the undergrowth of self-deception. So please remember to believe in yourself, believe in the intention, believe in love – and the magic will work.

Ritual to Attract the Quality of 'Romance' Itself

Whether we're looking for love for the first time, as an antidote to a series of mediocre dates, or perhaps after a relationship that ended badly, we're hopeful that we'll find the connection and happiness that we deserve. But in magic work it's not necessarily a person that you are calling out to, but the essence of romance itself, its energy and its secrets. When love comes to you in the form of another human being, it cloaks you both in its mysterious embrace.

This ritual will allow you to conjure and encourage romantic love in your life.

Peitho was one of Aphrodite's handmaidens. She was identified as the Greek goddess of persuasion, seduction, enchantment and guile, and was usually depicted with a dove and a ball of twine – symbols of binding someone to you (the twine) with your charm (the dove). By petitioning Peitho, romance may come unexpectedly, or you may find you start to seek it out purposefully. You might grow in confidence when it comes to flirting with enticing strangers, enjoy a series of great dates, or simply believe more in the possibility of love – this ritual will invite the essence of romance into your life.

You will need:
a piece of paper and a pen
6 rose quartz crystals
a 2ft length of gold twine or ribbon
an image of a dove

1. On the piece of paper write:

    'With Peitho's charm and love divine,
    I invoke romance by pen and line.'

2. Place the image of the dove over your verse, and then five of the rose quartz crystals around the dove in a pentagram.
3. Coil the twine or ribbon around the crystals to seal your intention. Finally, place your last piece of rose quartz on top of the dove and say:

> *'Romance is welcome in my life.*
> *With rose and dove and golden twine,*
> *Invited here to fill my soul.*
> *With all of Peitho's magic words,*
> *Enchanting now her wit and guile,*
> *To lure romance here with a smile.'*

Leave the petition until the next full moon, and you will attract romance into your life.

Wish for a New Love

Now you have invited the spirit of romance into your life, you can also wish for the type of person who will embody its essence.

In European folklore, blowing on a dandelion seed head was used for many magical objectives, such as making a wish, to divine how many weeks or months it would take for the wish to come true, or to foretell the time it would take for a lover to woo you.

On a windless, early morning of a waxing moon phase (and at the time of year when dandelions are flourishing in your local environment), go out into an open space where you can be sure of finding dandelion seed heads.

Sit down beside a seed head without disturbing it and close your eyes. Think about the type of person you would most like to meet and describe their best qualities, their interests, and the way they would act in a relationship. You may want to visualise them, or perhaps you can hear their voice or feel their presence.

When you have experienced this visualisation for a moment or so, open your eyes and make your wish.

Say: 'I wish for this person to come into my life. How long will I have to wait to meet them?'

Now blow on the dandelion head until all its seeds are dispersed, counting the number of breaths it takes as this number will signify how many months it will take to meet your heart's desire.

Cupid's Arrows – Love at First Sight

Cupid is well known for shooting his arrows at two unconnected people, resulting in a moment we call 'love at first sight'.

I think nearly all of us have experienced some form of this before, and it's a truly magical feeling. When we are struck by Cupid's arrows, it can be a moment of pure physical attraction – or a deep soulful connection, as if we are looking into the eyes of someone else's soul (usually mirroring our own). We might not even speak to this person for a while – or ever again. Some of the most memorable love arrows connect us to the stranger who smiles at us on a plane, or someone you share a fleeting glance with when your eyes meet across a street.

However, if you would like to experience a mutual love at first sight moment, and nurture this feeling of instant attraction into something more, perform this ritual on a full moon night.

RITUAL FOR MUTUAL ATTRACTION

You will need:
The Two of Cups tarot card
a red candle
rose essential oil
a rough ruby or garnet
a piece of paper and a pen

1. Carve your name down the side of the candle. Light the candle and let it burn down into your name while you perform the rest of the ritual.
2. At a safe distance from the candle, place the tarot card on your piece of paper and draw two symbolic arrows on the paper – one to the west of the card and one to the east. Then place the crystal on top of the card. Drizzle a little of the rose essential oil on the crystal to consecrate your ritual.
3. Focus on the candle flame for a minute or so, then say:

   'These arrows point to lovers fair,
   Who see each other once, then dare
   To fall into the well of love,
   Where water's blessed by gods above.'

4. Remove the crystal, hold the tarot card to your heart for a moment or two, then replace it between the arrows and leave it in place for one lunar cycle. Blow out the candle.

5. Once the ritual is complete, carry the crystal with you to help your love at first sight moments evolve into meaningful connections.

A Ritual to Capture the Attention of a Crush

We've all had a crush on someone who just doesn't seem interested or hasn't even noticed us, but maybe you don't want to give up on them just yet. There are generally two ways to deal with infatuation (deriving from a Latin word meaning 'make foolish'): you can either choose to let go and move on or give your crush your best shot first. This ritual will allow your feelings to be known and will encourage your crush to notice you, if there is a potential romantic spark.

This ritual is best performed during a waxing moon phase.

You will need:
a bowl of water
a rose

1. Gently trace your name and that of your heart's desire on the surface of the water with the rose – if you don't know their name write 'the desired one'.

2. Then hold the rose stem to you, and say:

> *'With Aphrodite's blessing, my crush for someone*
> *is crystal clear as this water.*
> *Yet if they do not wish to engage in my desire,*
> *then I will let go and move on to*
> *someone else.'*

3. Throw the rose into the water to seal your intention.

4. Leave overnight, then in the morning pour away the water and bury the rose in a quiet outdoor spot.

5. By the next full moon, if the person concerned has still not noticed you, then you will be able to let go of your infatuation and move on.

DESIRE TEST

Aphrodite was renowned for seductive powers that could captivate lovers both mortal and divine. However, there are very few of us who share her unwavering confidence when it comes to a new romantic relationship, so it's normal in the early stages of seeing someone to worry whether the other person is as invested as you are. You may obsessively check your phone and wonder why there have been no texts or calls, agonise over every little word you've said and convince yourself that maybe they're not interested after all. When you're in a cycle of worry, sometimes all you need is clarity, so here's a simple practice to test if the other person is genuinely into you.

This ritual is best performed on the evening of a waxing moon.

You will need:
a ring
a 2ft length of gold thread or fine twine
a red candle
a piece of paper and a pen

1. Light the candle, and on the paper write the name of your admirer. Thread the ring onto the twine, tying together the ends so that you have a pendulum.
2. Hold the pendulum over the name on the paper with your elbow resting on the table and gaze into the candle flame for a minute or so to find stillness. Then turn your gaze to the name.
3. Be patient. The ring will start to swing of its own accord (due to the tiny involuntary muscle movements in your arm that are resonating with the universal energy that flows through you). As it starts to swing focus on the name. Note in which direction the pendulum is swinging.

   • Clockwise: the person you like needs more encouragement to get closer.

- East to west: they are interested in you.
- Anti-clockwise: they aren't interested in you in a romantic way.
- Back and forth (away from, and towards you): they share your feelings, but aren't sure of how you feel.

A RITUAL TO KINDLE ROMANCE WITH SOMEONE YOU ALREADY KNOW

Often we can develop an attraction to someone we've come to know well through family, friends or work. We may wonder if they are as interested in us as we are in them. To find out and encourage them to see you in a more romantic light, use this lunar folk charm.

This ritual is best performed on the night of a full moon.

You will need:
a clear quartz crystal
jasmine essential oil
ylang ylang essential oil
sweet almond oil

1. Take the clear quartz crystal and drizzle on some of the jasmine and ylang ylang essential oil.
2. As you do so say:

    'By the light of the moon I'll seduce you now,
    With the crystal's truth I will draw on its power,

You will come to me now, inspired by this spell
With jasmine and ylang ylang to drink
    from the well.
The magical waters will keep you entranced,
And bring us together united in dance.'

3. Hold the crystal up to your eye and gaze at the full moon through it. If you can't see the moon, then hold the crystal up to the sky and say: 'If the moon sees me, then I see the moon, for clouds do not detract from her presence.'

4. Keep the crystal with you and whenever you meet with the person that you're interested in, hold it tight in your hand for a few seconds to inspirit you with the moon's energy. If within one lunar cycle they do not reciprocate, then you will know it's time to retract your intention. Simply cleanse the stone with sweet almond oil, and use it only when you have the same intention towards someone else in the future.

A RITUAL TO ATTRACT A LONG-TERM SPECIAL SOMEONE

The Norse goddess of love, Freya, was thought to wear a magical love necklace known as the Brisingamen, which some say was made up of exquisite amber stones. This glorious 'crystal' (it's actually fossilised tree resin) is known for its static electrical effect when rubbed vigorously, attracting particles to its surface. It's hardly surprising it has been used as a crystal for attraction spells.

Here's a ritual to ensure that if you're looking for a long-term relationship, you attract the right kind of person, someone truly compatible with you. For this reason, you need to think carefully about what you are looking for before you begin this spell.

Start this ritual on a Friday evening (Freya's day) to activate the amber and decide what you truly desire.

You will need:
a piece of amber
a pink candle
a white candle
a piece of paper and a pen
rose essential oil
patchouli essential oil

1. Light the two candles: pink to represent love and white to represent you.
2. Then make a list of ten basic qualities that you desire in your special someone.
3. When you have finished, write the word AMBER above the list, and the word LOVE below the list.
4. Now drip two drops each of the essential oils onto the paper to seal your intention and place the amber at the centre of it. As you do so say:

'With amber's gold charm and my
    heartfelt desire,

My search is beginning to light love's own fire,
By rose and patchouli, I send out my wish
To find the right one who brings more
       than a kiss.
But loving and tender, then true and forever,
This amber will bring me the right kind of lover.

5. Now drizzle a little more of the rose and patchouli essential oils onto the amber, and then leave everything in place overnight.
6. In the morning, fold away your wish list and keep it somewhere safe, and make sure to keep the amber with you for one week. The following Friday repeat the charm, and within two more Fridays someone special will be in your life.

A CHARM TO ENCOURAGE EXCLUSIVITY

Once you have met your match, you may feel uncertain of their commitment. Maybe you're worried that if you start acting like you're a couple, they'll run a mile? Here's a simple charm that will encourage you to put your own feelings first and bring you closer to exclusivity.

You will need:

a mix of flowers that includes at least three of the
    following: roses, gardenia, lilies, gladioli, lavender,
    agapanthus, sunflowers and alliums. (You are going to

create a magic circle around you with your flowers,
so you will need more than just a handful!)
12 pink tourmaline crystals

1. Find an outdoor sanctuary, a place where you can
    feel at one with nature and where you know you
    won't be disturbed.
2. Cast a magic circle by scattering your chosen
    flowers around you.
3. Form an inner circle using the pink tourmaline,
    making sure each of the crystals is evenly spaced.
4. As you stand in the centre of your magic circle, say:

    'Protected by this circle blessed,
    My love will be secure and set,
    With tourmaline and nature's gifts,
    They will be true and never drift.'

5. Spin round once in an anti-clockwise direction,
    stop, and then take up the nearest piece of tour-
    maline to you. Keep it under your bed for at least
    one lunar cycle to encourage this person to be true
    to only you.

TRANSFORMING ROMANCE TO COMMITMENT

In Celtic lore, the knotted wood found in willow tree
branches was thought to have been braided by spirits
or fairies. To cut the tree down or lop off one of these

precious branches would bring bad luck. However, if you stood before a sacred willow knot and braided your hair with your love's, your romance would be strengthened. This adapted knotting spell will help to transform any ongoing love relationship into a long-term commitment.

You will need:
a handful of willow leaves (or images of willow leaves)
3 x 2ft lengths of white ribbon
3 strands of finest white cotton braided to
    symbolise your hair
3 strands of finest red cotton braided to symbolise your
    partner's hair
rose essential oil
a silk pouch

1. Knot the three ribbons and the two lengths of 'hair' together.
2. Braid the three ribbons, plaiting in the cotton threads as you go along. Once you've reached the end of the braid and secured it, you can sprinkle on a few drops of the rose oil.
3. As you do so say:

> *'This rose oil seals my heartfelt desire,*
> *By willow's magic knots will rise,*
> *Twist now the braid and bind forever,*
> *These two souls locked in love's only treasure.'*

4. Place the braid in the pouch with the willow leaves, and leave in a safe, secret place to petition your desire for long-term love.

THE RELATIONSHIP ORACLE

To discover where this relationship is going, how your partner feels about you right now and what they secretly want for the future, use this simple divination technique.

This ritual is best performed on the evening of a full moon.

You will need:
12 large crystals to represent the astrological elements:
3 pieces of red carnelians (Fire)
3 pieces of yellow citrine (Air)
3 pieces of blue lace agate (Water)
3 pieces of green jasper (Earth)
a very small piece of tumbled rose quartz

1. Create a zodiac circle with the twelve crystals. Begin at a west point and work anti-clockwise in this order red, green, yellow, blue – taking care to make sure that the crystals are evenly spaced.
2. You are going to ask three questions:

   • What does my partner think about me right now?
   • What do they secretly want?
   • Where is this relationship going?

3. Cast the rose quartz crystal into the middle of the circle, and whichever crystal it falls nearest to will give you the answer to the first question.
4. Repeat the same process for the next two questions and see below for the oracle replies.

Red stones

Answer to question 1: they see you as someone independent that can at times be challenging to have around, but ultimately they love your spirit.

Answer to question 2: they want to date, but not get too serious.

Answer to question 3: this relationship will work if you go with the flow.

Yellow stones

Answer to question 1: they think you're fun to have around and seem very easy-going.

Answer to question 2: they want to communicate more as a couple and be more honest.

Answer to question 3: a spontaneous, non-committed relationship that could develop into a deeper connection if neither of you put too much pressure on things.

Green stones

Answer to question 1: they think you're quite realistic, mature and down to earth when it comes to love.

Answer to question 2: they want to take your relationship to the next level.

Answer to question 3: a long-term commitment is possible, if you both maintain your individual ambitions.

Blue stones
Answer to question 1: they think you're very sensitive, spiritual or mysterious.
Answer to question 2: they want things to carry on just as they are.
Answer to question 3: a potentially intense love affair, but the long-term future is uncertain.

Repeat this oracle at every full moon, the answers may of course change, but that is the nature of relationships too.

AN ENCHANTMENT TO MAINTAIN DESIRE

Eos was the rosy-fingered Greek goddess of the dawn; she poured morning dew on the land and opened the golden gates of heaven for the sun god, Helios, to ride his golden chariot across the sky. Her affair with Aphrodite's lover, the god Ares, enraged Aphrodite, who cursed Eos with insatiable lust for mortal men. Among the men that Eos seduced were the Aeolian prince, Cephalus, and the Trojan prince, Tithonus, but despite her many love affairs she was always true to her lovers. Eos is called upon to keep the flame of desire burning, and to ensure you will become closer to the one you love.

This ritual is best performed on the evening of a new crescent moon.

You will need:
a small pouch
a piece of amber
an acorn
a silver ring
a key
an image of the sunrise
2 lodestones
a red candle
a piece of paper and a pen

1. Light the candle and place the image of the sunrise in front of it. Place the amber, acorn, ring and key in your pouch and secure it, before placing it on top of your sunrise image.
2. Place the two lodestones one on either side of the candle. (These stones are 'magnetic' so align them to a north/south axis to enhance their qualities.)
3. As you gaze into the flame, focus for a moment on your desire for never-ending passion between you and your named partner.
4. Now write this magical verse on a piece of paper, then say it aloud:

> *'With rosy-fingered dawn my light is set,*
> *Her golden chariot brings me pleasures yet.*
> *When Eos' dewdrops fall beneath her brow,*

With silver ring and keys to join us now,
And all the world awakens to her song,
Then this desire be locked, forever bound.
The stones will draw us closer, two to one
With candle red, our love won't be undone.'

5. Blow out the candle once you have focused on maintaining your mutual passion.
6. Every evening until the full moon, move the two lodestones closer and closer to the unlit candle until on the night of the full moon they are both touching it.
7. Light the candle to seal your intention.

From then on mutual physical desire will continue for as long as you want this charm to work.

LETTING GO AND MOVING ON

So the romance fizzled out, the text messages stopped and you felt quite bereft and unsure of what went wrong. Perhaps you thought, 'Was it something I said or did, or didn't say or do?' Being let down or disappointed, even in the early stages of a relationship, is not easy to get over. We can feel totally rejected and that doesn't help our self-esteem at all.

This ritual will help you restore self-worth, thanks to the beneficial enchantment of Aphrodite, who knew her own worth and valued herself more than anything. It will also prepare you to invoke new romance when you're ready to move on and start dating again. Letting go of the dream of what could have been and the memories isn't easy, but Aphrodite's shrine to self-value will help you get through difficult times.

This ritual is best performed on the evening of a waning moon.

You will need:
an image of apples
an image of roses
an image of doves
a handful of seashells
5 rose quartz crystals
5 rhodochrosite crystals
a pink candle
a small hand mirror
a piece of rough ruby or garnet

1. Find a space where you can create a small shrine to Aphrodite. It's best to pick a quiet corner of your home, as the shrine will need to stay in place for at least one lunar cycle.
2. Start putting together the shrine by placing the images, shells, and pink crystals in a circle with the candle placed at the centre. Place the mirror nearest to you, alongside the ruby.
3. Light the candle and gaze into the flame for about thirty seconds. Then pick up the mirror and focus on your reflection and say:

> *'Mirror, mirror in my hand*
> *I am the fairest in this land,*
> *Of Aphrodite's rosy bower,*
> *Where I restore my self-worth vow,*
> *True to myself to heal my wound*
> *Now forgiving all that's flowered.'*

4. Put the mirror down and hold up the ruby as close as you can to the candle flame as you say:

> *'With roses and myrtles, let love lost be gone,*
> *With mirror and goddess, I leave all that's done,*
> *With crystals and candles, we burn out the past,*
> *And take up this charm to make new love that lasts.'*

5. Finally, place the ruby back on the shrine so that it can be charged with Aphrodite's magical power overnight. Keep the stone with you as a romantic charm wherever you go until next full moon.
6. You will begin to forget about your previous relationship, self-value will be restored and you will be ready to attract new romance your way, if you feel ready.

AN UNBINDING SPELL FOR UNWANTED ATTENTION

Love can play tricks on everyone, and that means someone else may be struck by Cupid's arrow, but you find it hard to reciprocate those feelings. They are into you and even though you've politely tried to make it clear that you're not interested, they just won't let it go. Here's a way to untie the knot that has them bound to you.

You will need:
a white tea-light candle
a black tea-light candle
a photo of the admirer, or their name written on paper
1 x 2ft length of black ribbon
1 x 2ft length of white ribbon

1. Light the candles, the white represents you and the black, your admirer. Place their photo or the piece of paper with their name on it in front of the black candle.
2. Take the two ribbons and knot them together at one end, and then make three more knots before knotting the ends together so that you have a total of five knots.
3. Hold each end of the knotted ribbons and pull gently so the length is taut and say:

    'Knot one undone will cast my spell
    Knot two undone unties their will,
    Knot three undone releases me,
    Knot four undone alone I'll be,
    Knot five undone breaks down their urge
    All knots untied and all is purged.'

4. Now untie each knot, and then roll up the paper or photo and wind the ribbons around it.
5. Blow out the white candle as you say: 'All your desire or hope be gone, I am free.'
6. Blow out the black candle and dispose of it as far away as possible from your home, along with the ribbons and the photo/slip of paper.

You will now be free of your admirer's unwanted attention.

A Spell to Understand Someone's Intentions

There are times when you become complacent about a relationship without meaning to. It might be that you're busy and forget to prioritise the other person, or that you stop making the effort because you're so used to them being in your life and, somewhere along the line, it hasn't worked out. Instead of thinking about all the things you could have done, or berating yourself and thinking, 'What's wrong with me?', take action and use this spell to test whether they might still be interested in you, and how to try and reconcile if they are.

You will need:

2 teaspoons of orrisroot powder
2 large deciduous tree leaves (oak, beech, birch, etc)

1. Go out into nature, preferably where there are woods, parkland, trees, and find yourself two fallen leaves from any tree of your choice, or gently pluck the leaves from your chosen tree. Scratch on the surface of each leaf your name and the other person's.

2. Sprinkle the orrisroot powder over the leaves, and then throw them into running water (a stream, river or any stretch of moving water).

3. Say: 'When these leaves reach the sea, intentions are revealed to me.'

If either leaf immediately sinks, then the spell is broken, but if they stay afloat then there is a chance that you might be able to reconcile your differences with time.

Attracting a Soulmate

Many of us believe we have a soulmate or twin flame out there somewhere, and if only we could find them it would be the perfect relationship to make our dreams come true.

Yet, in some ways, a true soulmate is rather like a mirror, a person who shows you everything about you – both the positive and negative – helping you to grow into your most authentic self. The connection is often instant, a feeling of having perhaps known the person in another life. However, you may find after many moons that because you are so similar and in sync with your soulmate that they can begin to drive you up the wall!

If you are unwavering in your desire to meet your soulmate, perform this ritual during the evening of a new crescent moon.

You will need:
2 red candles
2 pieces of red carnelians or red jasper

1. Light the two candles and place next to each other.
2. Hold the two crystals in each hand and say:

   'When twin flames burn they share a light,
   That reaches into darkest night,
   They know each other through and through,
   A recognition, mirrored too,
   Of red stones burnt in earth's deep time,
   These souls refined now unified,
   So bring together hand in hand
   And join their magic in this land.'

3. Return the crystals to the table one in front of each candle, and very carefully bring the two candles even closer together. Imagine the candles merging and the flames beginning to burn as one.
4. Blow out the candles when you intuitively feel the candles burning as one and keep the stones safe to attract a soulmate or twin flame into your life.

Chapter Six

Honouring Enduring Love

'You have absorb'd me. I have a
sensation at the present moment as
though I was dissolving.'

Letter to Fanny Brawne, John Keats

After the whirlwind first months of a new relationship,
love settles in and unites couples with a force more powerful than just physical desire. But transitioning from a 'me'
into a 'we' can sometimes feel daunting, and you have to
ask yourself whether your futures are aligned — do you

want the same things in the long-term, and are you well suited ideologically?

Do we accept that love is perhaps testing each of us to see beyond the illusions of our romantic projections? Can we see how to love another person without making them feel responsible for our happiness? This is where some of us get cold feet, while others realise they've found someone they're meant to be with.

In this chapter you will discover ways to help and enhance this journey towards a sense of fulfilment and commitment. I have included a mutual binding spell, if your partner is a willing participant and wishes to commit completely to a relationship. Otherwise there are rituals to encourage faithfulness, to protect your relationship, rituals to maintain long-term commitment, and enchantments to help heal the wound of a broken heart. Most of all, these charms will nurture your relationships and give love a chance to flourish and grow in your magical garden.

A SPELL TO ENCOURAGE FIDELITY

Trust is the foundation of any long-term relationship. When you don't trust your partner, it can take a huge toll on your mental and emotional wellbeing and affect your other close relationships. While you can't force yourself to trust someone – trust is built over time through words and actions – you can encourage honesty and fidelity between you and your partner. This spell calls on the powers of Fides, the Roman goddess of faith and trust, to protect your interests and ensure your partner (and you) remain faithful to any mutual promise.

This ritual is best performed on the evening of a full moon.

You will need:
a piece of lapis lazuli
a rough ruby
a jar
rose water
hibiscus flower essence (or jasmine if unavailable)
distilled witchhazel

1. Place the jar along with the ingredients in your chosen sacred space. Fill the jar with a mixture of half rose water, a quarter witch hazel and a quarter flower essence.

2. Stir the liquid for ten seconds, then place the lapis and the ruby into the water. Say:

    'Bejewelled in rubies, cloaked in gold
    She glides like goddesses of old,
    Of lapis stone and woven threads
    Of magic moons and all that's said.'

3. Put your hands around the jar and then say:

    'Now Fides comes to bless desire,
    And keep us close but light our fire,
    Between two lovers cast this spell,

To weave us ever in the well
Of deepest love where none will turn
Their head to others, our love to burn.'

4. Seal the jar and then place it on a window ledge to absorb the power of the moon.
5. The next day, remove your two crystals and keep them under your bed so that both you and your partner can be protected by the power of fidelity.

A MAGIC CIRCLE TO HELP SUSTAIN ROMANCE

When you're completely in love, you feel soothed and at peace when you're with your partner. This magic circle will help to strengthen those positive feelings and allow your relationship to continue to flourish. The magic circle can symbolise the perfect unity of your love.

This ritual is best performed on the evening of a full moon.

You will need:
12 red tea-light candles
12 pieces of rough emerald
patchouli essential oil
1 x 3ft length of red ribbon, cord or thread

1. Find a quiet, private spot outside if possible; if that's not possible, try to be near an open window so that you're able to draw on the power of the

moon. Create a magic circle around you by placing
an equidistant circle of the candles, and in between
each candle a piece of emerald.

2. Symbolically light the candles (imagine in your
mind they are lit to safely perform this spell) and
then stand in the middle of the circle, take up the
ribbon and wind it around and around your wrist
as you say:

'Nurture our hearts to this my tryst,
To flourish now our precious gift,
In Aphrodite's circle found
We're safe from all who steal around,
Take up this stone now touched with oil
No person will our love despoil.'

3. Now take up one piece of emerald, drizzle the
patchouli oil over it to anoint it, then hold it
close to your heart while you repeat the incantation. Find stillness for a moment, and then leave
the circle and put the emerald in the centre to
replace you.

4. Leave overnight, and your charm will be sanc-
tioned by the universe.

A MUTUAL BINDING SPELL

You may be lucky enough to have a partner who believes
in making things happen through magical means too. If

so, you can perform this mutual binding spell to confirm your intentions for the future.

The Roman naturalist and philosopher Pliny the Elder believed that magnetite (a natural magnet) was discovered by and named after a shepherd called Magnes. When walking across Mount Ida, the shepherd found that his iron-heeled shoes clung to the rock on the ground, which led to the discovery of the mineral. As a result of its natural magnetic properties, magnetite – or lodestone – was often used in ancient attraction spells to ensure a faithful partnership.

This magnetite charm will only work if you both acknowledge and consecrate the powerful bond between you.

This spell is best carried out on a sunny day.

You will need:
2 lodestones (magnetite)

1. Take your two lodestones (you carry one, your partner carries the other) and go out into the countryside. Find yourself a quiet, private place, that will allow you to feel like it's just the two of you at one with nature.
2. Sit down cross-legged facing each other with you facing south and your partner facing north, if possible, to align the stones to the magnetic poles of the Earth.
3. Simultaneously, hold the stones up to your third eye chakra (midway between your eyebrows) and

both say: 'I affirm my trust and love is your trust and love, and my lodestone is a symbol of our mutual goals and intentions.'

4. Then exchange lodestones slowly by placing yours in the hand of your partner and taking theirs in your hand, as if you are holding hands. You may feel the magnetic resonance of the stones as you do so.

5. Now, simultaneously, both hold the gifted lodestone up to your forehead and repeat the above affirmation to seal your intention.

6. Keep your lodestones separate on your journey home, and then place together in your home to symbolise your mutual direction forward.

A Charm to Encourage Commitment and Growth

If you truly believe your current partner could be 'the one' or vice versa, this spell will support your relationship and allow you to remain committed to one another and continue to grow together.

There are many lovely unifying traditions that pre-date our traditional concept of marriage. In paganism, handfasting was an important ritual whereby a length of cloth or ribbon was tied around the hands of lovers to promote fertility and fidelity. In ancient Greek folk religion, lengths of twining plants such as vine leaves were put forward as offerings to the sun god, Helios, at dusk. Then at dawn, a poem or spell would be recited and Helios would appear to transform the bindings to gold – a sign that the love they represented had now been made sacred – and the hand-fasting ceremony would begin.

This charm is best performed as the sun sets. You can perform this on your own, but if your partner is happy to perform this spell with you, it will encourage exclusivity, long-term commitment and mutual growth.

You will need:
sandalwood incense or diffuser
a 1ft length of red ribbon
a 1ft length of gold ribbon
a ring (preferably set with a garnet or other red stone)

1. Tie the red ribbon around your ring and then do the same with the gold ribbon, crossing the knot over the first knot. Tie together the ends of each ribbon so that you have one red loop and one gold loop.
2. Lay your loops out flat on a table and light the incense or diffuser for atmosphere.
3. Place the looped ribbons over your hands, so one loop passes over your left hand and one over your right hand. Close your eyes and say:

'Now Helios comes to bless these binds,
His golden love will make us shine,
And we'll be safe to grow as one,
And be united by the sun,'

4. Remove the loops from your wrists. (If your partner is taking part in this ritual, they should now carry out the above steps.)

5. With the ribbons still tied round the ring, place under your bed overnight. In the morning, take up the looped ring and place it in a special box and keep in a safe place.

6. This ritual will allow you to progress towards the kind of commitment that you're both looking for.

MAINTAINING THE SPIRIT OF ROMANCE IN A LONG-TERM COMMITMENT

If we identify Selene as the whimsical, flighty goddess of romance, we can accept that romance might leave us just as quickly as she comes to us. But for a longer-term commitment to work out there needs to be mutual respect and acceptance, and we must learn to love ourselves rather than get tangled up in frivolous games with our egos. When you live with someone and spend a vast amount of time together, you're bound to find faults because no one is perfect. If you're both tired and there's a pile of dishes in the sink waiting to be cleaned, it's easy to be snappy and resentful in the moment. However, it's the underlying love and connection that you share that will always bring you back together and have you going from exasperation to adoration.

To focus on the big-picture romance, rather than the niggly daily frustrations, perform this enchantment to conjure the spirit of the lunar goddess of love, Selene.

This enchantment is best performed on the evening of a waxing moon.

You will need:
a mirror
rose essential oil
ylang ylang essential oil
a piece of moonstone
a handful of rose petals

1. If possible, place the mirror in a safe, secret place outside where it can reflect the night sky to draw down the energy of the moon. Drizzle two drops of each oil onto the mirror, and then sprinkle the rose petals on top. Finally place the moonstone on the mirror and say:

    'Now draw down the moon and Selene's power,
    So her spirit returns here to lighten our bower,
    Delighting by day, the cup overflows,
    Of moonstone, romance and the smell of the rose.'

2. Leave this in place until the full moon, and you will bring Selene's spirt of romance back into your love life again.

A Secret Shrine for Love to Grow

When the passion fades we must find other ways to love one another. Or rather other ways for love to settle in between us to reinforce mutual respect, honesty, under-standing and appreciation for each other's differences. To grow this kind of all-encompassing love between you and someone special, create your own secret shrine. This is a place where love grows and needs little tending except your awareness.

This ritual is best performed on the evening of a waxing moon.

You will need:
25 white/grey stones, rocks, shells or crystals
a permanent marker
a large rhodochrosite crystal
a moonstone (to activate lunar energy)
a sunstone (to activate solar energy)
a red candle

1. Using fifteen of your stones or shells, build a shrine perhaps in the shape of a pyramid or any geometric shape you fancy or find easiest to do. The main thing is to acknowledge it as your garden shrine to love. (This can be inside if you don't have access to an outdoor space.)
2. Write one of the following magic words on each of the remaining ten stones to grow love:

Love
Please
Accept
Give
Forgive
Nurture
Support
Grow
Evolve
Trust

3. Balance these ten stones on the top of your shrine, and finish off with the moonstone, sunstone and rhodochrosite.

4. Light the red candle, stand before your shrine and say:

'This garden grows, as love it flows,
This love it grows and seeds are sown,
In loving words my heart is fixed,
In loving stones there'll be no rift,
My heart and yours is ever true,
This secret place for me and you.

Thank nature's growth for trusting here,
The sun and moon for love so clear,
The stones that see, the flowers that heal,
The moon and sun, and all that feel
The stars and sky, all held above
This garden grows to show our love.'

5. Every full moon evening say the above verse at your shrine to bless your relationship with flourishing and consistent love.

A Posy to Improve Physical Chemistry

Although we might talk about the physical side of our relationships less often than the emotional aspects, it is incredibly important too. Sexual affinity is a key part of any relationship, so this enchantment posy is designed to bring renewed physical passion between you and your partner.

Orris root powder was used in many ancient grimoires (magical texts) as the base for elixirs and love potions to stir lust in men's hearts. It derives from the rhizome of various species of iris flower, and when matured has a deeply evocative fragrance of violets. It is a prized base note in perfumes and has an incredibly sensual scent. Use it to stir a little chemistry into your love life too.

You will need:
a mirror
2 red candles
1 pink candle
3 red ribbons
jasmine essential oil
patchouli essential oil
a pinch of orris root powder
3 roses

1. Place the two red candles in front of the mirror. Dress the pink candle with the two oils by drizzling a couple of drops down the side of the candle, and then sprinkle with the orris root powder.

2. Next, bind this pink candle by winding the red ribbons round and round it and then tying them into a bow. Place the roses behind the bow to make a posy.

3. Place the pink candle between the two red ones, and say the following as you focus on your reflection in the mirror:

> *'Patchouli brings us sensual bliss,*
> *While orris root the need to kiss,*
> *These candles red, the roses too,*
> *Will send us blessings, love renewed*
> *With jasmine, ribbons, posies be,*
> *Empowered to bring such intimacy.'*

4. Continue to gaze into the mirror while you focus on the positive joy of you and your partner's physical needs.

5. Seal your intention by leaving the posy in front of the mirror overnight, and let the magic begin.

A RITUAL TO RECONNECT

Sometimes it feels like the heady romantic, sensual intensity that you experienced when you first started dating your partner has worn off. But you still love your partner and want to nurture your love, so how can you rekindle those initial sentiments and get back on track? This ritual will support your desire to reconnect.

This ritual is best performed on the evening of a waxing moon.

You will need:
a fine braid made of three threads of black cotton or silk (about 6 inches long)
a piece of black tourmaline
vetiver essential oil

1. Wind the ready-plaited braid around your ring finger and fasten by pressing your middle finger firmly against it to hold it in place.
2. With your other hand, drizzle a little vetiver essential oil over the black tourmaline as you say:

   'Reconnect with lunar light,
   My heart is open from tonight,
   Take black stone and see the way,
   Take this oil and make a vow,
   Take this crystal all is won
   For love remains, the seal is done'.

3. Repeat this incantation six times (the number of harmony and stability), then open your fingers and let the braid unwind or fall naturally from your finger.

4. Take the black tourmaline and kiss it to seal your intention. Then wind the braid around the black tourmaline.

5. Leave the tourmaline on a window ledge overnight to absorb the energy of the moon and open your heart to reconnecting with your lover again.

AFTER THE STORM

Despite our best efforts, sometimes relationships just don't work out – and that can be incredibly painful. Opening ourselves up to someone else, whether physically, mentally, emotionally or spiritually, can leave us vulnerable so you need to take time to grieve, heal and let go. Surround yourself with your friends and family and focus fully on your wellbeing.

Once you feel ready, you can try this restorative ritual which will help you to dispel any negative feelings towards yourself and your ex, and hopefully go some way to healing any lingering wounds of the heart. When you are mentally and emotionally prepared, you can then move on to the next ritual about forgiveness and compassion. The most important thing is to go at your own pace and don't push yourself to move on, if you're not ready to.

You will need:
an apple
a paper bag

a large stone
a piece of paper and a pen

1. On the paper, write down the name of the person you've split up with. Go ahead and fill the piece of paper – write it over and over again to purge the name from your mind.
2. Now cut up the apple into tiny pieces and put the pieces in the centre of the paper with the stone.
3. Wrap the paper around and twist it together at the top to seal your intention.
4. Place the wrapped apple in a paper bag then go to a river, lake, or fairly fast-flowing stream, and throw the paper bag into the water (the paper will disintegrate, but if you prefer, you can throw just the wrapped apple into the water and take the bag home for recycling). Watch as it sinks to the bottom.
5. Over time the apple and paper will rot (simultaneously your feelings will also diminish and fade away). As you walk away, see how walking away from a rotting apple is not unlike walking away from a relationship that ultimately wasn't right for you. It will feel liberating.

A Forgiveness and Compassion Grid

In Roman mythology, Cardea (sometimes mistaken for the goddess Carna) was a goddess who protected door hinges.

Cardea was invoked to prevent evil entering the home, and hawthorn – her sacred flower – was hung around door hinges to protect children in their cradles from evil spirits. Ovid remarked that 'she opens things that have been closed, and closes things that have been opened'. In this sense she not only protects us, but opens our hearts to see the truth of what is behind our own closed doors, and can offer guidance when bringing closure to a difficult relationship.

Forgiveness and compassion are perhaps the two most valued qualities of love, and to feel both requires integrity and honesty. The hardest thing in our pain is to forgive and send compassionate energy to someone who has hurt us.

Here's how to embrace and connect to Cardea's magical force when you need closure, by working with compassion and forgiveness.

You will need:
3 rose quartz crystals
3 pieces of rhodochrosite or rhodonite
3 aquamarines
3 moonstones
a pink tea-light candle
a handful of hawthorn twigs, flowers or leaves

1. Create a grid in a place where the stones won't be disturbed. Create a heart shape by alternating your crystals, making sure that everything is evenly spaced out. Finally, place the pink candle in the middle and surround it with a ring of hawthorn.

2. Sit before your grid, and first focus on how you value and love yourself, giving warmth and genuine care to who you are and how you are an incredibly special person.

3. Focus on the qualities of forgiveness and what it means to forgive, and what it means to truly care for someone else, without expectations.

4. Then visualise the other person in your life who you need to either forgive or be more compassionate towards. Visualise the warm energy flowing from this heart to their heart chakra, and connecting back to your own heart chakra, creating a circuit of caring energy. Take up each crystal in turn, hold it to your heart chakra and then return it to the grid, while you say: 'With this stone I bring compassion [or forgiveness] to this relationship.'

5. Repeat this ritual every full moon until you begin to feel you no longer need to perform it and have found your own closure.

WAKE UP FROM A BREAK-UP RITUAL

The Greek hero Theseus was aided in his quest to destroy the deadly Minotaur at the heart of the labyrinth by the Cretan princess Ariadne, who fell in love with him. Ariadne gave Theseus a ball of twine so he would be able to retrace his steps and escape the maze. Ariadne eloped with Theseus and sailed to the island of Naxos, but the hero then abandoned her. Ariadne was found by the god Dionysus and subsequently married him. This story illustrates that although we might think we've met the person meant for us, their actions can prove that they're not worthy of our love. Instead, their role in our life was to lead us on a journey to the right person.

With Ariadne's ball of thread, you too can begin to see that someone better will be out there for you – someone who is meant for you and you alone. This is when a break-up becomes a wake-up call.

This ritual is best performed on the evening of a waning moon.

You will need:
a ball of string or twine
16 pieces of red carnelians or rough rubies
a small box

1. Find a quiet space, preferably outside to connect more easily to the lunar energy as it draws away any painful feelings.
2. Place the sixteen crystals in rows of four with each row about two inches apart.
3. Take the ball of string and start from the top left to right, and begin to weave it up and down between the crystals on the top line, then round and back from right to left along the same line, then move down a line and repeat. Keep moving down the lines until you have woven the string around all the crystals in all four lines.

4. Leave the ball of string beneath the four lines and say:

> *'The labyrinth's secret I was told,*
> *Is love the one whose hand you hold.*
> *Yet with this twine I leave the place*
> *Where all seemed perfect in the chase.*
> *Yet hidden lies and lightless dark*
> *They fooled me, lest I left too fast,*
> *Now crystals trace my way from woe,*
> *This twine will show me where to go.*
>
> *With crystals four by four I rise*
> *Above the fear of this lost prize,*
> *Which never was but just a chance*
> *To lead me on a merry dance,*
> *But as I walk the labyrinth now*
> *Retrace my steps and leave somehow,*
> *I find my dark heart turns to light*
> *And wakes up to my truth so bright.'*

5. Now pick up each crystal in turn, leaving the twine exactly as it is, and place them in the box. Keep the box in a safe place to ensure your future love will be loyal and true.

6. Hold the end of the twine (the ball end) and gradually wind the twine back on the ball, as you slowly draw it from its labyrinth-like shape.

7. As you do so, visualise yourself finding your way out of the labyrinth and out of the fear, the

hurt, the anger, the loss. You are now waking up to loving yourself, knowing that your positive wake-up call will bring you the love you genuinely deserve.

WATER LILY MOVING-ON SPELL

We never really get over a break-up or loss, but rather we get *through* it. At first we may feel overwhelmed with grief, anger, or a need for some kind of revenge. Some of us may date on the rebound as a way to numb the pain, others resolve to live single lives, fearful of being hurt again. But being true to yourself is about accepting what's been and what will be, and moving on with courage and self-belief.

If we can truly love others from afar – and are genuinely happy that they have found love or joy, even if we are not part of that happiness, we will discover how to love ourselves better in return too. This ritual will help you to do exactly that.

When we feel stuck in the murky depths of love's darkness, we're not unlike the water lily, which rises from muddy banks and slowly grows towards the sunlight. Similarly, you too can rise up above the clouded waters and move into the light again.

You will need:
a favourite image of water lilies
3 white candles
a mirror

1. Place the three candles in a triangular formation in front of your mirror, with the north point of the triangle closest to the mirror. Carefully light them.

2. Put the image of the water lilies in front of the candles so that you can see it reflected in the mirror.

3. Find stillness, and gaze into the reflection of the water lilies and the candle flames. Be mindful of how, like a water lily, you will emerge from the dark and grow into the light.

4. Blow out the candles to commit your intention to the universe that you will grow like a water lily and move on and up.

BEING SINGLE AGAIN – A DANCE PARTNER RITUAL

Although this chapter is about romantic relationships, there are times when we may prefer to be single. It's important to remember that the most incredible relationship we can have is the one with our self, so here's a spell to celebrate being single and to rejoice in your free spirit.

Go out into the countryside and dance with the world!

Choose your dance partner carefully. It can be anything that catches your eye – a scudding cloud, a swaying tree, a nodding daffodil. Or it can be all of the world and nature. Follow your dance partner's 'moves', sway like the tree, bend like the corn, sing to the birds, look up at the clouds, smile back at the faces in rocks, or wave at the light that plays on water. Dance with the water too, as if you were a ripple, a wave, a dolphin, a swan.

Take great joy in your newfound dance partner, for the world itself is a magical dancefloor. If you waltz a little with Mother Earth, you'll discover that love is truly all around you and flows through you, and you don't need to rely on anyone else for that magic to happen.

After your dance, write down the verse below and read it aloud to remind you that the love you find all around you in nature is as animating as the love you find in another human being.

> 'When our bed is filled with grief,
> We walk alone, a silent thief.
> When our love is wrenched from us,
> We dance among the morning dust.
> When we don't know where to go
> Our dreams remind us how we were,
> And all above the lies we're sent,
> We wonder at the life that's dreamt,
> But dancing in the world at large,
> I feel the love of nature's arms.'

Chapter Seven

Cherishing Friends and Family

'Piglet sidled up to Pooh from behind.
'Pooh,' he whispered.
'Yes, Piglet?'
'Nothing,' said Piglet, taking Pooh's
paw. 'I just wanted to be sure of you.'

The House at Pooh Corner, A.A. Milne

Love for a friend (*philia*, see page 4) is selfless and has no
hidden agendas. Friendship is the ability to share, to accept
your differences, to respect each other's boundaries, and

to never judge the other person. A close friendship allows you to be completely yourself without fear that you might not fit in – it heals you. Family love (*storge*, see page 5) is the instinctive bond between parent and child, as well as the supportive love relationships between siblings, cousins and other family members, and also clans and groups.

So whether you want to love and protect your family and home to the best possible ability or enjoy the affinity of a kindred spirit, this chapter offers you rituals and spells to call on and promote the forms of love where we support others, accept them for who they are, and open ourselves to a true sense of acceptance.

MUTUAL RESPECT CHARM

Here's a charm to help you maintain a good relationship with the people in your life by boosting mutual respect and acceptance.

This charm is best performed on the evening of a waxing moon.

You will need:
2 yellow candles
2 small amethysts
2 x 6in lengths of yellow ribbon
2 oak leaves or acorns

1. Place the two amethysts in front of the two candles, and then create a circle around each piece of amethyst using the ribbons.

2. Hold the acorns or leaves, one in each hand, and say:

'This ritual opens me to love that's clear and
    loyal and true,
For letting someone be themselves, and not
    forgetting, too.
Respect both ways and different views, and find
    connection there,
A pathway through the tangled trees, for
    friendship true and fair.'

3. Place the acorns in the circle with the amethyst and leave everything in place overnight to charge the crystals with acorn's respectful, individualistic power.

4. Take the crystals with you next time you meet up with a friend to inspirit the relationship with loving acceptance of both your individual selves.

BEST FRIEND BONDING RITUAL

Best friends can fall out – maybe due to silly disagreements about anything from a choice in a new date, or perhaps because of what someone said or didn't say, did or didn't do. But this ritual will allow you to maintain a strong friendship with a specific person, and encourage you to be a better friend.

This ritual is best performed at a full moon.

You will need:
a rose quartz bracelet
a citrine bracelet
a pink tea-light candle
a yellow tea-light candle

1. Place the rose quartz bracelet around the yellow candle, and the citrine bracelet around the pink candle.
2. Light the candles and concentrate on your desire for you and your best friend to never fall out over trivial things, to never feel alone, and make a promise to offer them your unwavering support. Say:

   'These friendship bracelets make us strong,
   With crystals threaded for our bond,
   No words will hurt, no thoughts will stain,
   For honest love is our refrain.'

3. Let the candles burn down a little before you remove the bracelets. The next time you see your friend, offer them the bracelet as a symbol of your beautiful bond of friendship.

Attracting a Kindred Spirit

A kindred spirit is a like-minded soul with whom we share similar values and perspectives on life. When you meet for the first time, they might feel strangely familiar – as if you've met before in another life.

Kindred spirits are free from expectations, and they usually care enough about each other to give the other all the space they need. They come together, part their ways, and may meet up again months or even years later, and carry on where they left off.

So if you want to attract a kindred spirit into your life, here's how.

You will need:
4 pieces of citrine
4 pieces of rhodochrosite
a piece of clear quartz

1. You are going to call on the four directions to summon a kindred spirit to you. The spirit winds in Greek mythology embodied qualities of the four main winds in the northern hemisphere. So the north wind was cold, testing; south was warm, teasing; the east was cool, bracing; the west was comforting, embracing.
2. Place the four pieces of citrine so that they mirror the compass points, north, east, south and west. Then place the four rhodochrosite between each point, before placing the quartz in the middle.

3. Find stillness and focus on your desire for a kindred spirit. Take the central quartz crystal and hold it to your heart chakra (mid-chest) and say: 'I ask these winds of change, north, east, south and west, to bring me a kindred spirit, so that we understand and accept one another in every way.'

4. Leave your magic grid in place until the following new moon to attract a kindred spirit into your world.

RECONCILIATION

Sometimes we fall out with those we're closest too, perhaps because we care more about our opinion over anyone else's. We may agree to differ, but secretly seethe with resentment, then huff and puff and build a smokescreen around our true feelings. And if we do, sometimes we end up losing that friend for good. So here's a way to help patch up a relationship that may have turned sour. This ritual will help you both to see the way forward to reconciling your differences.

The paradoxical nature of oud (see page 53) is that the heartwood only exudes this aroma when infected by a harmful fungus, and so from something that is potentially threatening to the tree comes a beautiful essence. Similarly, when we feel threatened by a difficult relationship, we can magically manifest a positive outcome.

This ritual is best performed on the evening of a full moon.

You will need:
an oud-based perfume or oud essential oil
a sandalwood incense stick
a piece of selenite
a piece of blue lace agate

If you have easy access to an outdoor space, then perform this ritual outside. If not, you can use a window ledge or a spot close to the window to draw down lunar energy.

1. Place the selenite and blue agate next to each other.
2. Light the incense, and for about a minute, focus on the person with whom you want to reconcile. Think about all the positive things you have felt for them in the past. Visualise yourself in the future, both laughing and enjoying each other's company again with no bad feelings.
3. Drizzle two drops of the oil onto the crystals and say:

   'With precious oud we'll find our way,
   To reconcile our different days,
   With selenite we'll clear the air,
   And agate blue will find us near.'

4. Move the two stones closer so they are now touching. Continue to reflect on the positive feelings and experiences you shared with your friend.

5. To seal your intention to reconcile, hold a crystal in each hand and knock them gently together three times.

6. Snuff out the incense, and leave the stones touching one another overnight.

By the next full moon, you will be on the path to making up with this person.

CELEBRATING TRUST

As social creatures, it's natural for us to want to share our lives with the people around us, and it's important to know our friends truly have our back and can be trusted with our most intimate beliefs, secrets, fears and desires.

This ritual will promote trust between you and those friends you know are loyal and true.

You will need:
5 white tea-light candles
3 pieces of amethyst
3 pieces of rose quartz
3 piece of blue lace agate

1. Place the candles in a circle, light them carefully then surround with the crystals in this order: one amethyst, one rose quartz, one blue lace agate and so on.

2. Focus on the candles and perhaps notice the light dancing in the crystals, showing you that the love and trust between you and your friends is always there if you choose it to be.

3. Say: 'With these crystals we build our trust and strengthen our bonds. With these flames we grow together, not apart, and will always be there for one another.'

4. When you feel ready, blow out the candles and leave the grid overnight to charge the energy of trust between you and your friends.

GRATITUDE GARLAND

Giving out love to friends and family is just as necessary as accepting it. We need to send the people around us our love and support and give gratitude for our shared connection, so that they know we appreciate and respect them. Love given freely will inspire others to love freely. What goes around, comes around.

This gratitude garland can be placed or hung in any space that you share with family or friends.

You will need:
a red ribbon
5 rosebuds with stems (cut short as you're going to insert them into the braid)
5 lavender flowers (again cut short)
5 bay laurel leaves

a 2ft length of braid made of natural twine
basil essential oil

1. Take the braided twine and shape into a circular garland, securing the ends with the red ribbon.
2. Insert the flowers and laurel leaves along the braid, weaving the stems into the braid to ensure that they're secured.
3. Finally anoint the rosebuds with the basil oil and say:

'This garland gift will show the way,
To gratitude for all each day,
As love it flows out from this charm,
To bring each one a sense of calm.'

4. Leave the garland in your chosen place to stir a little love magic into your environment and give gratitude to those who deserve to be cared for.

Warm Wishes Ritual

Family relationships are often the most difficult to deal with, mostly because we didn't choose these people consciously as our friends. We may have different beliefs, ages and lifestyle choices, we may live worlds apart, and the only thing holding us together is the blood tie. This medieval knotting charm will help you to share love and warm wishes with anyone you find it difficult to relate to. This doesn't mean that you have to suddenly go out socialising with anyone who's hurt you, or feel beholden to them in any way, but instead it will allow you to wish them well from afar.

This ritual is best performed on the evening of a waxing moon.

You will need:
4 pieces of black tourmaline
4 pieces of citrine
3 lengths (each about 2ft) of yellow ribbon
a yellow candle
tea tree essential oil
a 2ft length of gold twine or cord

1. Light the candle, and braid the yellow ribbons.
2. Once your plait is finished, place the black tourmaline to the north and south of it and the citrine to the east and west of it.
3. Anoint the braid with two drops of tree tea oil to purify and promote harmony.
4. Finally, wind the gold twine or cord round and round the braid and tie the ends of the cord.

Leave this charm in a discreet place by the main entrance to your home to promote family harmony.

BANISH NEGATIVE ENERGY

Our home is filled with different energies, some vitalising, some loving and some negative. When the negative energy from a home starts to overwhelm the people living in it, it can create a stressful, tense environment. So to banish all psychic negativity from your home, place this crystal grid in a secret place where it won't be disturbed. It will also sustain all forms of good feelings and thoughts towards others.

You will need:
For the invocation:
an opal
a small bowl of spring water
frankincense essential oil
a pink tea-light candle

For the grid:
4 rose quartz crystals
an opal

1. Begin by lighting the pink candle. Close your eyes and centre yourself in the moment to find stillness. Focus on all the goodness you would like to give out in your personal world, and how you want to protect your family from negative psychic energy.
2. Open your eyes and place the opal in the water. Then drop a little of the frankincense oil onto the water. See how the oil separates and sits on the

surface of the water? Think about how you can separate the negative energy from the positive.

3. Take hold of the opal and gently swirl it round and round in the oil to imbue it with the frankincense's harmonious power. The opal is now dedicated, and ready to be used in the grid.

4. Find a secret place to assemble your protection grid. Place the opal in the centre surrounded by the four rose quartz crystals, one to the north, south, east and west. Say:

'With opals pure and frankincense,
Rose crystals banish all that's tense,
To exile all that wrongs our right,
Enhance good feelings day and night.'

5. Leave the grid in your sacred place all year round to banish negative energy and encourage empowering love.

A VOTIVE TO PROTECT HOME AND FAMILY

Throughout pagan religions it was believed certain deities and spirits, such as Hestia, the Greek goddess of the hearth, and the Lares, house spirits of Roman tradition, would protect the home to bring harmony, good luck and success for all who lived there. Similarly you're going to create a small votive to the Lares of your home to bring you beneficial energy.

You will need:
a small bowl
6 basil leaves
6 sage leaves
a cinnamon stick
lemon verbena essential oil
3 large pieces of black obsidian

1. Place the basil leaves in the bowl and then form a second layer of sage leaves.
2. Place the cinnamon stick on top of the herbs and aligned to east/west.
3. Finally, place the three crystals in a triangle shape on top, with one crystal to the north, one to the south-west, one to the south-east.
4. Drizzle over a few drops of the lemon verbena oil as you say: 'Thanks be to the spirits of this house to love and protect us all from negative energy, and to bring us happiness and wellbeing in all we do.'
5. Leave your votive near the main entrance of your home and each time you pass touch the stones to be empowered with beneficial energy from the spirits of the household.

FAR AWAY LOVE

Family can end up in all corners of the world, so when we are far away from loved ones we need to remember not only to keep up on a social level through texts and calls, but also to nourish our shared spiritual, magical connection. This ritual enables you to sense that however far away you are from your loved ones, you can feel each other's warmth and love reciprocated.

You will need:
a world map
a piece of labradorite
2 white candles

1. Carefully light the two candles and open up the world map.
2. First locate and point to the place where your loved one currently resides. Close your eyes and then begin to move your finger in a spiral, working the spiralling larger and larger around the map until you reach the edges.
3. As you do so, think of your loved one, see them in your mind, visualise them happily talking to you, or imagine yourself with them in this place far from you.
4. Open your eyes and now place the labradorite on the place on the map where they are currently living.
5. Say: 'With this crystal my love is sent to you [name]. This energy brings you support, comfort, protection and an eternal connection in our hearts and souls.'

6. If you both perform this ritual at the same time, you will be surprised by how powerful the sense of psychic connectivity will be between you, filling you both with love and positivity for the future.

AWAY FROM HOME – LOVE ON YOUR TRAVELS

It's all very well receiving and giving love to those we know well, but there are times when we set off into the big wide world alone and need to feel that we will be protected and cared for en route. Here's a way to ensure love is all around you, wherever you go.

Along the waysides and crossroads of ancient Greek thoroughfares, *herms* (stone pillar with the carved head of the god Hermes) were placed as signposts and a symbol of good luck for travellers. *Herms* were often found in front of houses and were consecrated with olive oil or adorned with garlands of flowers. They could also be made from piles of stones that became popular additions along the roadside, warding off the evil eye or protecting travellers from danger. As someone walked past a *herm*, they would add their own stone to it ensuring Hermes' protection.

Here's a way to receive genuine love and kindness when you are on your travels, knowing that you will be protected by the good luck magic of Hermes.

This ritual is best performed on the evening before you set off on your travels. If you can, find a crossroads or a country lane where there is no traffic. If not, perform this ritual in your own home where there is a transition from one room to another, or an angular corner of two walls to represent the 'crossroad'.

You will need:
a few handfuls of pebbles or stones
4 drops of frankincense essential oil (the number 4 is
    sacred to Hermes)
a handful of mint leaves or stems
a piece of black tourmaline.

1. Stand facing north and pile up a miniature shrine of pebbles and stones, building them up into a rounded heap or a pyramid shape.
2. Anoint the shrine by drizzling the frankincense oil over the stones, and then sprinkle over the mint leaves.
3. Place the tourmaline on top while you say:

    'With Hermes care my way is shown,
    Where strangers pass and all is known,
    We smile across the sacred shrine
    To always know this love divine.'

4. Blow a kiss to the shrine to seal your petition to Hermes. Make sure to take the tourmaline with you on your travels, and leave the rest of the shrine in place.

Every time you embark on a long journey, if you have time, return first to this place and add another stone or pebble to the pile to ensure you meet the best people and receive Hermes' good luck.

PART THREE

Universal and Mystical Love

'Love possesses not nor would it
be possessed: for love is sufficient
unto love.'

'On Love', Kahlil Gibran

Poets, mystics and spiritual and esoteric authors have written extensively about a kind of divine love that transcends and permeates all – universal love. Perhaps the best way to understand its essence is through the words of twelfth-century CE mystic Hildegard von Bingen, who wrote: 'Love abounds in all things, excels from the depths to beyond the stars, is lovingly disposed to all things. She has given the king on high the kiss of peace.'

Love is the sun's rays warming our cheeks, the way a willow tree bows down to a river, the song of a chaffinch in spring, or it can take the form of a close familial bond, a kindred spirit, a creative passion. It's love that allows us to experience a mysterious sense of wonder and awe when we engage with the natural world. This is because love has woven its way into all of our lives, and is part of the very fabric of our planet. It is the golden thread in the tapestry of universal energy, and the essence of the divine that animates all things.

When we draw on love's mystical power in our magic work, we can return the favour and give back to the planet by reciprocating and spreading the love we have received. This next section will offer ways to engage and connect to universal love and its many mysteries. The more you surrender yourself to the power of love, the more you can love yourself in the process.

Chapter Eight

Connecting to Mystical Love

'My heart leaps up when I behold
A rainbow in the sky'

'My Heart Leaps Up',
William Wordsworth

Around the sixth century BCE, the ancient Greeks (as did other ancient civilisations) named the then known planets after their gods. The planets became the representatives of the gods, and each planet was associated with the symbolic qualities of its own god. For example, Venus – then known as the 'star of Aphrodite' – was associated with love, while Mercury – then known as the 'star of Hermes' – was associated with trade and trickery.

Whether we believe in the gods or not, we still look up to these, our nearest stellar wanderers, to help us reconnect to the universe whether through arts such as astrology, or just the belief there is something mysterious, divine, or numinous at work 'up there' among the planets, stars and far beyond.

The cosmos is indeed a magical place, and we can honour and love it for what it is by starting with the love of our own planet and the two most important, vitalising influences on the Earth – the sun and moon.

THE EARTH CARE

This ritual can be performed at any time of day, apart from sunrise and sunset, to allow you to connect to the Earth's natural energies.

You will need:
patchouli essential oil
an image of a pentagram
5 pieces of smoky quartz
5 pieces of bark from a tree
5 pebbles or stones

1. Go outside and find a quiet, private place. Sit comfortably on the ground – to really connect to

the earth, sit cross-legged, keeping your hips and shoulders aligned and back straight.

2. Place the pentagram before you and place one of each crystal on each of its points, then do the same for each piece of bark and each pebble. In the centre of your pentagram, pipette five drops of patchouli oil.

3. Close your eyes and take in the fragrance of the oil, and also the nature surrounding you. Notice your contact with the ground and reach out your fingers and touch it. Be aware of the tangible influence of the world around you.

4. Come out of your mindful awareness, and say: 'Thank you, Earth, for supporting me in all I do, and with love I give back to you all I can.'

5. Stay in the moment for a minute or so, then collect your Earth votives and keep them in a safe place to reuse for this purpose only, whenever you need to feel connected to the planet and give it some love.

THE SUN EMBRACE

Many ancient civilisations worshipped the sun and followed its daily journey across the sky, believing it to descend to the underworld when night fell. The Greek god of the sun was originally Helios, but was later identified with Apollo, the god of light. It is Helios' power that you are going to draw on so that your own solar light can shine through and radiate solar love to the world.

One tale of Helios recounts how he fell in love with a mortal princess, Leucothoe. Utterly enamoured with the princess, Helios rejected all of his former lovers, including the nymph, Clytie. Incensed upon learning of the sun god's betrayal, Clytie took revenge by informing Leucothoe's father, Orchamus, of the affair. Humiliated by what he saw as the defilement of his daughter, Orchamus buried Leucothoe alive. Although Helios was too late to save the princess, he poured an elixir onto her grave and she was transformed into a frankincense tree. Clytie's fate, however, was less pleasant. Rejected by Helios, who never forgave her, all she could do was gaze at him as he crossed the sky in his chariot. Eventually Clytie faded away and became the purple flower heliotrope. (Both heliotrope and frankincense were used in ancient Greek love spells to conjure the god's favour.)

This ritual will allow you to harness the solar light's love that energises everything on this planet.

This ritual is best performed at either sunrise or sunset.

You will need:
a heliotrope flower, or an image of one
frankincense essential oil
2 sunstones

1. Find an outdoor space where you won't be disturbed and where you can bury your crystals safely. Place your flower on the ground and place the two sunstones (to represent you and the sun) on either side of it.

2. Drizzle a little of the frankincense oil on the crystals to seal your intention to give and receive love from the sun.

3. If you're using an image, fold the paper around one of the crystals. If you're using a real flower, bury it together with one sunstone. Say: 'I am blessed by the sun's light, which will shine through me every day so that I can give out my own loving light to the world.'

4. Take the other sunstone with you and keep in a sunny place in the home to bring you the sun's luck and love.

The Moon Wish

Among the gravitational influences on the Earth, it is the moon that has the most powerful effect on our tides and oceans. The lunar cycle provides us with potent times to harvest, sow, finalise projects or find new love (see the glossary for lunar phases). Although the moon's light is not her own, she synthesises the sun's reflective light with her own energy. To reach out and draw down the moon's nurturing energy, make a wish with the moon and you'll be blessed with her goodness.

This ritual is best performed on the evening of a full moon.

You will need:

4 moonstones (to represent each phase of the waxing, full, waning, and dark of the moon phases)

4 sage leaves

a pouch

a pin

1. Hold each sage leaf close to your heart in turn as you repeat your wish.
2. Place the leaves on a window ledge and place one moonstone on each leaf.
3. Wait until after the full moon has passed, and during the waning moon remove one moonstone. Read aloud the wish, bury the leaf, and keep the moonstone in the pouch.
4. Repeat the same process during the dark of the moon with the second moonstone, and again during the next waxing phase with the third moonstone, and finally the fourth moonstone at the next full moon.

Over one lunar cycle, you will have drawn down the moon's power to fulfil your wish and to connect to her protective love.

DAILY NATURE CONNECTION RITUAL

The more you show you care for the world around you daily, the more you will feel a sense of being embraced by it too. Participating in nature, whether smelling a rose, running through the surf, stroking a cat, or smiling at the faces in the clouds, brings you a deeper connection to the sacredness within you.

Here's a quick practice that you can use on a daily basis once you have found yourself a special space to visit in nature.

Prioritise a time when you will go outside every day to commune with nature. Whether you step out into the garden, find a green space in the urban landscape, or have the countryside on your doorstep, make it an intention to do so. Set an alarm on your watch or phone and treat it as you would a tea break – time to put down tools and be enchanted by life.

Stand tall, centre yourself, find stillness and choose a distant object or view to focus on. Take in what you see before you, then gradually focus on what you see in your peripheral vision. What do you smell, hear, sense, feel? Be aware of these sensations and thoughts. By focusing on what you see, you'll become more aware of what you feel and what is going on around you.

By being mindful of your own reactions, your connection to the natural world will grow stronger every day, until you feel so much a part of it that you realise you are participating in nature's grand design. End this mindful awareness by putting your hands together in prayer and giving thanks to nature for bringing you closer to her loving embrace.

A TRYST WITH TREES

For thousands of years, trees have been worshipped, celebrated and respected for their magical influence in our lives. The word 'dryad' (a wood nymph) is rooted in an ancient word for a tree, in particular, the oak tree. Ancient Greek rites to summon the aid of the dryads were performed secretly within oak tree glades. So with this in mind, embark on your own secret meeting with an oak tree and the dryads. Show them your love and respect and you will be given their blessing that will allow you to be as strong and steadfast as they are.

Trees speak their own language so listen to their rustling leaves on a breezy day, hug a tree whenever you feel inspired to do so, or put your ear to the bark; you'll be surprised to learn what they're saying to you.

This ritual is best performed as early as possible in the morning to align to the sun's rising influence.

You will need:
a piece of paper with the incantation below written on it
a piece of malachite
a piece of citrine
an oak tree

1. Stand beneath the oak tree and place your hands on its bark for about a minute to experience its energy permeating your hands.
2. Then read the spell out loud to the tree:

'Love wakens us, blows golden kisses across the
        misty air,
While morning doves sip dew beneath some
        silver pears.
Disguised as dawn she lifts the cloak of
        darkest night,
Bejewelled in cool citrine, she paints the
        morning light.
As Venus then, she finds a lovers' tryst,
Then twists their fate, to make them lose
        their grip,
And carve their names on oak trees they embrace,
It's then they see love's staring in their face.'

3. Pick up the two crystals and hold them against the bark for a minute to give out their power to the tree, but also to draw in the oak's energy.

4. Before you go, say: 'Thank you, mighty oak, for your gift of love's strength, this tryst is our secret to keep for ever.'

5. When you feel intuitively that the stones have absorbed the tree's power, put them in your pocket so that you can keep them with you for the rest of the day. Then leave them in a safe place in your home to radiate protective energy all around you.

LOVE FOR BIRDS, FAUNA AND THE WILD WORLD

Loving the world around you means you have to accept all aspects of it too, and that means loving the birds, the fox, the newt, the bat, the ant, the bee and any other wild thing that comes to mind. Here's a simple celebratory gift of love to connect to the wildness of nature by calling on the well-known lunar goddess of beasts, hunting and the forests – Artemis. Although all wild animals were sacred to her, she was particularly associated with deer, bears, boars and hawks, who accompanied her as she sped through the skies in a gold chariot drawn by four golden stags.

This ritual is best performed on the night of a full moon.

You will need:
an image of the new crescent moon
cypress essential oil
a large red candle
2 opals

1. Place the symbol of the new crescent moon on a table, and write around the outside of the moon: 'The moon she grows to fulfil my wish, this lunar light brings me Artemis' gifts.'
2. Light the candle and place it behind the symbol.
3. Drizzle a little of the cypress oil onto each opal, and place them in front of the moon symbol. Say:

'Artemis of the enchanted moon
Bless me now with a guided tune,
Wild love connected with flickering flames,
As I sing your song for nature's refrain.'

4. Focus on the opals for about thirty seconds as the candle burns down a little. Then hold both opals up to the sky and affirm, 'With these stones my way is set to embrace and love the wildness of life so that it may return that love to me.'

Keep the stones with you to bring you happy connectivity to the wild world around you.

SEA SALUTATION

The ocean usually fills us with wonder as we gaze across it from the safety of the shore, but sometimes, if we're adrift on the open sea, it might fill us with dread instead. Our oceans' hidden depths are full of mysteries, challenging adventurers, explorers and the curious to discover its beauty and treasures.

This simple sea salutation will bring you closer to the powerful energy of the oceans, which cover about 70 per cent of the Earth's surface. Show your respect and align yourself to their lunar-influenced depths of love.

You will need:

a beach

a bag

1. Purposefully go beach-combing at low tide. Depending on the beach, look for shells, stones, pebbles or even small bits of driftwood. Anything that attracts your eye. You'll be using these to create a magic circle, so when you feel that you've collected enough of the beach's treasures, find a pleasant spot to sit and take a break. The idea is for the tide to wash away your magic circle later in the day, so make sure you pick a spot that will be caressed by waves.

2. With your collected items, create a magic circle. If you're on a sandy beach, then in the centre of the circle draw a pentagram with your finger or a stick; if you're on a pebbly beach, place five pebbles or shells to mark the five points.

3. Stand and face the sea with your hands at your chest in prayer, then sweep your arms up to the sky, around and back to your chest. Repeat three times slowly and say each time:

   'I came and found a treasure today
   Now given back to ocean's way.'

4. Leave your ritual offering on the beach, knowing that the sea will reclaim it and spread your

affirmation of love to the deepest, hidden depths of the planet.

A JAR OF ENCHANTMENT

If we respect and care for plants, flowers, herbs and all kinds of botanicals, they will reward us with their beneficial influence. If you have a favourite herb or flower, then make sure to include it in this enchantment. The magical jar is filled with a symbolic balance of the four elements, to align you to the power of this mystical magic.

This enchantment is best performed on the evening of a waxing moon.

You will need:
a lidded jar
2 pinches of allspice
dried basil
dried mint
marigold petals
rose petals
a clove
dried sage
dried rosemary
a piece of amber
a piece of citrine
cedarwood essential oil
patchouli essential oil
a candle

1. Put all of your dry ingredients in the jar with the crystals, and gently stir around with your fingers. Drop one drop each of the essential oils into the jar and close the lid. Don't open it again until the full moon.

2. On the evening of the full moon, light a candle for ambience and open the jar. You may find the fragrance invokes thoughts, ideas or a sense of calm – reflect for a few moments on the contents and how it enhances your own sense of wellbeing.

3. Seal the jar and repeat the same process at each full moon to nurture the magical nature of plants and their connection to you.

Chapter Nine

Welcoming Divine Love

'But the day will come when you
will gather stones and stars as a child
plucks the valley-lilies, and then shall
you know that all these things are
living and fragrant.'

Garden of the Prophet, Kahlil Gibran

The rituals and practices in this chapter will open you
up to the sacred elements of divine love. The archetypal
essence of love moves through us mysteriously indeed. In

the words of St Paul, 'Love is patient; love is kind; love is not envious or boastful or arrogant or rude. It does not insist on its own way; it is not irritable or resentful; it does not rejoice in wrongdoing, but rejoices in the truth. It bears all things, believes all things, hopes all things, endures all things. Love never ends.'

In its divine way love comes to lighten our view, not darken our vision. So hold the light of yourself before your eyes and you'll no longer be deceived by your shadow.

SOULFUL PROTECTION

We may be busy attempting to reconnect to our deepest selves so we can experience a soulful flow of love and give it out to the world, but we need to protect ourselves from negative psychic energy before we embark on any spiritual work. Here are two ways to maintain a strong and unbreakable barrier around your psychic self. Perform this ritual not only to give you courage and strength, but to protect you from any form of negativity.

You will need:
4 pieces of black tourmaline
a piece of red carnelian
a piece of paper and a pen
pinewood essential oil

1. First, mark north, south, east and west on a piece of paper.

2. Place a piece of black tourmaline on each point and
    the carnelian in the centre. Say:

    'Protected now from all who dare,
    This grid will hold this soul so clear,
    With tourmaline a boundary's drawn,
    With stone so red, I'm kept from harm.'

3. Place the grid near the main entrance of your
    home and anoint it with a drop of pinewood essen-
    tial oil to create the protective boundary you seek.

A SOUL PROTECTION CHARM FOR YOUR TRAVELS

We need to feel safe when we are out and about, because
at times we are vulnerable and open to the big wide world.
This magic pouch will protect your soulful self from other
people's negativity and geopathic stress wherever you go.

You will need:
a silk or cotton pouch
a moonstone
a sunstone
a piece of malachite
a piece of citrine

1. These four stones represent the four elements of
    western astrology. To harness their power, hold

each stone in turn up towards the sky and say for each: 'This stone is now blessed by the protective energy of the cosmos.'

2. Keep them safely in the pouch and take them with you on your travels. If you ever feel a wave of indecision or a lack of focus or self-belief, take the stones out of the pouch and hold each one in turn and say: 'With this stone I am protected from all that is negative in this world, both the tangible and invisible.'

SPREADING LOVE AROUND – WHAT GOES AROUND, COMES AROUND

In magical circles, there is a belief that any intention cast into the world will always come back to you – and usually threefold. So, if what goes around comes around, then here's your chance to spread an authentic belief in the essence of love out into the world, knowing that love will come back round to you too.

You will need:
3 x 2ft lengths of gold twine or cord
3 pieces of rose quartz
3 pieces of celestite

1. Create two separate large triangles with your rose quartz and celestite – the point of the rose quartz

triangle should face north, while the point of the celestite south.

2. Knot together your three pieces of gold twine or cord and then braid the strands. Secure your braid with another knot, before making three more equidistant knots along the braid so that you have a total of five knots.

3. Wind the braid between the two triangles to form a figure of eight shape. As you do, say:

'Thrice times I send this spell-work round,
Thrice times I pull the knots unbound,
Compassion, grace and gratitude
This spell is cast to spread it too.'

4. Pick up the braid and now untie the three middle knots you have made. It might not take you long, or it might take you some time. What matters is that you are engaging in the ritual of unfurling compassion, grace and gratitude to the world as you do so.

AUTHENTICITY ORACLE

Being authentic – in other words being true to the deepest part of oneself – isn't easy when we're surrounded by external influences and expectations. But if you act from that soulful place within, you will find yourself on the true path to fulfilment. Taking too much stock in the opinions and judgements of the people around us can lead us away from this authentic space; however, by aligning to the synchronicity of oracles and their connection to the universal energy, you can find your way back on to the path of becoming your true, authentic soulful self.

This ritual will align you to that inner place where you can hear the divine voice that speaks through you, and know which path is the right one to follow. According to the principle of synchronicity, events that occur at exactly the same moment, especially seemingly random events, reveal something common to that moment – and this apparent coincidence is no longer merely down to chance, but has meaning to us personally. You can therefore discover a truth in the moment in relation to yourself, as the divine shines this symbolic light into your life.

You will need:
a large thick book (such as an encyclopaedia, Bible, dictionary, etc.)
4 dice
a white candle
a piece of paper and a pen

1. Prepare your question or issue that needs to be resolved to align you to your true pathway.
2. Shake the dice as you focus on your question, and when you intuitively feel the moment is right, toss the dice on the table.

3. Close your eyes and randomly flip open the book without hesitating; don't open your eyes, just touch either the left or right page. This will be the page with the oracle message.

4. Read the passage on that page associated with the numbers on the dice. For example, if you threw a two, a five, a three and a six, count sixteen lines from the beginning of the page, as this is where your oracle begins. The words you read may instantly mean something to you, but don't worry if they don't. Take a note of them on your piece of paper, and look out for signs and symbols that relate to the oracle in the following days.

Practise this divination technique whenever you have a question you want answered and feel that you can't find that authentic sense of direction. This will connect you to the synchronicity of the universe and to the part of you that intuitively knows what you should do.

ENHANCING YOUR PSYCHIC CONNECTION

To be able to truly flow with love's energies in the world, you can also draw on your innate psychic power, no matter how far away it seems from the realities of everyday life.

Crystals and gemstones are believed to store the archetypal knowledge that we all share in our collective unconscious. This crystal spell will help you to revive and become more aware of your connection to this hidden place.

This spell is best performed on the night of a full moon.

You will need:
a lidded jar
a piece of moldavite
a piece of labradorite
a piece of celestite
ylang ylang essential oil
frankincense essential oil

1. Half fill the jar with spring water and gently put in the three crystals.
2. Add one drop of each oil onto the water and watch it separate (this symbolises the separation of your psychic self from your logical being). Close the lid and leave the jar on a window ledge so that it can be charged with the moon's energy overnight.
3. The next day, dab a little of the potion onto your third eye chakra (midway between your eyebrows) to enhance your psychic power. Close your eyes, find stillness and centre yourself, being mindful only of your third eye and opening yourself to intuitive and psychic awareness.

You will find that over the next lunar cycle, your psychic awareness will grow and you will be more in touch with the deeper mystery within.

A Charm to Appreciate Mystery

In the words of the nineteenth-century Danish philosopher Søren Kierkegaard, 'Life is a mystery to be lived, not a problem to be solved.' With this in mind, you can truly connect to the mystery of life and love, and allow your hidden self to come alive.

Whether through passionate love, spiritual enlightenment or a moment of connection to the universe, this simple ritual will help you to appreciate the mysterious nature of love within yourself.

The Sator Square is a magic symbol, the earliest known example being discovered in the ruins of Pompeii. The message of this palindromic square can be read backwards as well as up and down, and still confounds experts to this day. Translated, it is thought to read: 'The Farmer Arepo works wheels', yet esoteric experts believe that the word 'Arepo' is a corruption of a Latin word meaning, 'creeps stealthily forward', and believe this is a deeply mysterious message.

You will need:
the Sator Square written on a piece of paper:
SATOR
AREPO
TENET
OPERA
ROTAS

1. First repeat the phrase over and over again, and backwards, at least nine times to instil a sense of mystery in you. Keep the magic square displayed where you can be aware of the words, the letters and appreciate its hidden secret. Don't try to decipher it or deconstruct it in any way, just let it be the mystery it is. This will help you to understand how love is a mystery too, to be cherished and experienced.

RITUAL FOR THE SACREDNESS OF ALL

Everything in the world is alive, every stone, every rock and every tree, imbued with the magical energy of the universe. But we often don't feel part of it, simply because our ego builds high walls to protect itself from the 'world out there'.

In this way we disconnect ourselves to become mere observers of what is around us and within us. But we don't have to just stand and stare at nature, the landscape, the clouds, the weather or the stars as if we are not part of it. To truly feel blessed and part of the universe, we need to participate in it and see that we take up not only a physical presence on planet Earth, but also a spiritual one.

Here's how to enjoy that experience and be part of the sacred nature of all.

This ritual is best performed on the evening of a full moon.

You will need:
a large clear quartz crystal
a large mirror
a white candle
rose essential oil

1. Sit before the mirror, place the candle in front of it and light it; hold the crystal with both hands. First gaze at your reflection and then at the flame dancing in the mirror.

2. After you are centred and have found stillness, turn your gaze to the crystal and look deep within it. This is a form of 'scrying', seeing patterns, colours or shapes in the crystal that you can interpret as an oracle. You may see the reflections of the candlelight, you may see yourself, you may see reflections of the shadows in the room, and you may see all of the universe if you look with your psychic sense. In fact, the longer you let your imagination engage with the crystal's depth, the more you will feel as if you are part of the crystal itself. If it doesn't work the first time and you don't begin 'to see' in a new way, try again the next full moon. Don't rush it. This moment of enlightenment will come to you at the right time.

3. When you come out of your scrying meditation, hold the crystal to your third eye chakra, and say the following words to affirm your dedication to participating and loving all that the universe is:

*'I see into the crystal as I see into the universe,
and as I see into the sacred depths of
myself, I see my soul.'*

4. Once you have performed this magical technique
    a few times, you will be more aware not only
    of your own soul self, but of the love that flows
    through you.

Last Words

Let's end this book by celebrating love's magic in all its forms.

Take your favourite crystal and purposefully go out into nature, perhaps arrange for a picnic, a beach meditation or just a great hike across the hills. Take with you a notebook, your phone or your journal, and as you walk, observe and jot down the things that feel meaningful to you. Maybe it's the way the wind blows through certain bushes or trees, a rustle in the hedge, a flock of birds, or a crawling insect.

Whatever it is that catches your attention means you are drawing on the beauty around you and experiencing awe and appreciation for it. If you love the landscape, you love the planet, the universe and yourself. There are no conditions, no judgements, just seeing that there is love in everything.

Now, in your mind, apply this sense of unconditional love to your relationships, to people, to the world at large, and to the mysterious nature of love itself.

Even when you truly feel this or know this experience, love may still at times run wildly past you, but it will also run with you. It may at times run ahead of you, but it will always turn back and find you again, even when you believe it might be lost for ever. Love will soften your heart and will give you strength to believe in yourself.

Before you head home, seal your intention to embrace and spread more love by holding up your crystal to your third eye chakra, and say:

> *'Where have you been since enchantment began?*
> *How many times have you danced on the sands?*
> *Where are the signs of your moonbeams at dawn,*
> *And how did you feel when the world was*
>   *not yours?*
> *Did you try roses to waken love's light?*
> *Or did you hunt wild ones to darken those nights*
> *When lust came and went like a*
>   *mesmerised beast,*
> *And serpents they hissed at the marriage-*
>   *less feast?*
> *So take up your crystal, anoint it with oil,*
> *Hold to your forehead and whisper this now,*
> *'Love comes to me now, Her song sung through*
>   *the world,*
> *With gold-threaded magic to cherish my soul.'*

Welcome, respect and give thanks to love, and its magic will be there for you, always.

Acknowledgements

My blessings and thanks as always go to everyone at Piatkus, especially Bernadette Marron, who helped to make this book so enchanting. I would also like to thank my family and friends (you know who you are), especially my daughter, Jess, for her loving support and for sharing so many magical moments with me.

Glossary of Correspondences

Here you will find suggested ingredients and other sacred resources; some are included in this book, and others can be used to replace those you may not have to hand, and can also be used to create your own rituals and spells. So for example, if you are in need of a new romantic attachment in your life, you would choose ingredients in the 'romance' list. You could light a red candle, place a piece of red carnelian before the candle and drop a little patchouli oil on the crystal while repeating a charm. You can also mix and match ingredients to reinforce various elements of your ritual or charm. But most of all, take pleasure and delight in the ingredients which will bring your own love magic to life.

ROMANCE
BOTANICALS
Basil
Bay
Gardenia
Jasmine
Laurel
Lavender
Lily
Mint

Orchid
Rose
Rosemary
Sunflower
Thyme
Vervain
Willow

CRYSTALS AND PRECIOUS STONES
Amber
Emerald
Garnet
Kunzite
Lepidolite
Lodestone (Magnetite)
Pink Tourmaline
Red Carnelian
Red Jasper
Rhodochrosite
Rose Quartz
Ruby

ESSENTIAL OILS
Frankincense
Jasmine
Lotus
Oud
Patchouli
Rose

Ylang Ylang

DEITIES
Aphrodite (Greek)
Eros (Greek)
Freya (Norse)
Hathor (Egyptian)
Inanna (Sumerian)
Kamadeva (Hindu)
Peitho (Greek)
Rati (Hindu)
Venus (Roman)

COLOURS (CANDLES OR OTHER VOTIVES)
Pink (romance, attraction)
Red (passion, sexuality)
White (purity, commitment)
Yellow (friendship)

LONG TERM LOVE/FRIENDSHIP
BOTANICALS
Bay Laurel
Lavender
Mint
Oak
Pine
Rose
Rosemary
Thyme

CRYSTALS AND PRECIOUS STONES
Aquamarine
Black Obsidian
Black Tourmaline
Blue Lace Agate
Citrine
Clear Quartz
Emerald
Labradorite
Lapis Lazuli
Lodestone (Magnetite)
Moonstone
Opal
Red Carnelian
Red Jasper
Selenite
Sunstone

ESSENTIAL OILS
Aloe Vera
Basil
Frankincense
Hibiscus
Juniper
Lemon Verbena
Oud
Patchouli
Sandalwood
Vetiver

DEITIES
Aphrodite (Greek)
Freya (Norse)
Helios (Greek)
Hera (Greek)
Parvati (Hindu)
Selene (Greek)
Venus (Roman)

COLOURS (CANDLES OR OTHER VOTIVES)
Black (reinforcement)
Brown (strength)
Pink (romance)
Red (empowerment)
White (purity
Yellow (friendship))

SELF-LOVE
BOTANICALS
Angelica
Bay leaf
Birch
Ficus
Lavender
Mint
Rose
Sage
Thyme

ESSENTIAL OILS
Cedarwood
Eucalyptus
Oud
Patchouli
Vetiver
Ylang Ylang

CRYSTALS AND PRECIOUS STONES
Carnelian
Citrine
Clear Quartz
Garnet
Malachite
Obsidian
Pink Tourmaline
Rose Quartz
Ruby
Sunstone

DEITIES
Aphrodite (Greek)
Apollo (Greek)
Artemis (Greek)
Brigid (Celtic)
Hestia (Greek)
Isis (Egyptian)

COLOURS (CANDLES AND OTHER VOTIVES)
Black (integrity)

Brown (conviction)
Green (manifestation)
Pink (love of others)
Red (self- belief)
White (purity)

SPIRITUAL/MYSTICAL LOVE

BOTANICALS
Ash, birch, beech or oak tree
Cherry blossom
Lavender
Lotus
Mint
Rose
Rosemary
Sage
Water Lily

CRYSTALS AND PRECIOUS STONES
Celestite
Citrine
Clear Quartz
Labradorite
Lapis Lazuli
Moldavite
Moonstone
Opal
Selenite
Smoky quartz
Sunstone

ESSENTIAL OILS
Clove
Cypress
Frankincense
Oud
Patchouli
Sandalwood

DEITIES
Arianrhod (Celtic)
Artemis (Greek)
Hecate (Greek)
Horus (Egyptian)
Isis (Egyptian)
Selene (Greek)

COLOURS (CANDLES AND OTHER VOTIVES)
Blue (intuition)
Turquoise (compassion)
Purple (spiritual awareness)
White (soul/divine connection)

Further Glossary

Greek/Roman Correspondences

Most of the Greek deities were assimilated into Roman civilisation and many of their Latin names are perhaps better known due to their association with the planets in our solar system. Here is a list of corresponding names. The rituals and enchantments in this book draw on the power of either the Greek or Roman deity, depending on the ritual's symbolic intention.

GREEK/ROMAN
Aphrodite/Venus
Ares/Mars
Artemis/Diana
Cronus/Saturn
Eros/Cupid
Hera/Juno
Hermes/Mercury
Hestia/Vesta
Ouranos/Uranus
Poseidon/Neptune
Selene/Luna
Zeus/Jupiter

Lunar Phases
The lunar phases are determined by the angle and the amount of the sun's light falling on the moon, plus the moon's angle to, or distance from, the Earth.

The main phases of the moon used in this book are as follows:

THE WAXING MOON (INCLUDES THE NEW CRESCENT MOON)

This phase lasts from the dark of the new moon to the full moon.

Perform charms and rituals for: progress, bewitchment, development, creativity, desire, new beginnings, romance, seduction, enlightenment, giving, revival

THE FULL MOON

Perform charms and rituals for: completion, fulfilment, intensity, passion, manifestation, decision-making, commitment, conclusion, purpose, intention

THE WANING MOON (INCLUDES THE WANING CRESCENT MOON)

This phase lasts from the full moon to the dark of the new moon

Perform charms and rituals for: releasing, letting go, dumping, giving up, banishing, recycling, endings

THE DARK OF THE NEW MOON

Perform charms and rituals for: restoration, acceptance, transformation, deliberation, reflection, reviewing, reconsidering, modifying

List of Chakras and Their Associated Energies

CROWN CHAKRA
Located: crown of the head
Energy: spiritual connection

THIRD EYE CHAKRA
Located: midway between the eyebrows
Energy: intellect, intuition and psychic sense

THROAT CHAKRA
Located: the throat and neck
Energy: communication

HEART CHAKRA
Located: middle of upper chest
Energy: love of self and others

SOLAR PLEXUS CHAKRA
Located: above the belly button
Energy: the state of one's ego

SACRAL CHAKRA
Located: lower belly
Energy: sexuality and feelings

BASE OR ROOT CHAKRA
Located: base of spine
Energy: how grounded we are; our basic survival instinct

About the Author

Sarah Bartlett is a professional astrologer and author of internationally bestselling books such as *The Little Book of Magic* series, *The Tarot Bible*, *The Witch's Spellbook* and *The Secrets of the Universe in 100 Symbols*. Sarah practises natural magic, tarot, astrology and other esoteric arts in the heart of the countryside.